# NATUROCRACY

for all beings

SHAUPAUN KOUMAR

ZORBA BOOKS

NATUROCRACY for all beings

Revised edition published by Zorba Books, January 2023
Website: www.zorbabooks.com
Email: info@zorbabooks.com
Author Name : Shaupaun Koumar

shaupaun@asia-europe-consulting.com

First published in January 2019 by the author

Printbook ISBN: 978-93-95217-22-4
Ebook ISBN: 978-93-95217-20-0



**Zorba Books Pvt. Ltd. (opc)**
Sushant Arcade,
Next to Courtyard Marriot,
Sushant Lok 1, Gurgaon – 122009, India

Printed in India.

# Contents

*In Memory of My Motherland*

*for the Young and Posterity*

# About the Author

Shaupaun Koumar (Kawsar), an engineer-turned-economist, was born on January 20, 1953, in old Dacca (Dhaka). He chose seamanship for his career in 1975 and received a scholarship to study Marine (Industrial) Engineering at the Marine Fisheries Academy in Chittagong, a very intensive academic course, which was run by Russian experts. He graduated from the academy in 1977 and immediately got an offer from the Libyan Ministry of Marine Fisheries. Before moving to Libya, he worked in a Japanese Shrimp Research Vessel in Chittagong for a very short time.

Shaupaun worked in Tripoli and Benghazi, Libya, for about three years, then abandoned his marine life. He moved to Belgium to pursue his Master's degree in a two-year Industrial Location and Development programme at the Vrije Universiteit Brussel (VUB). He graduated with distinction in 1990. In order to enrich the thesis of this programme entitled 'Economic and Ecological Impact of Tropical Deforestation', he simultaneously followed another Masters in Environmental Science (Human Ecology). He earned his second Master's degree in Management Programme from the same university in 1992.

He became passionate about applied economics and, in an unprecedented way (1994), enrolled in a four-year course at Vesalius College, VUB, to pursue a prestigious Bachelor's degree in an American-style education in Europe. He graduated from the university in 1998 with honours in Business Economics and a minor in Computer Information Systems. In fact, he has an insatiable hunger for knowledge about various academic disciplines.

He joined a consulting firm in Brussels as a Business Economist in 1998. Over time, he also specialised in Corporate Tax and Public Accounting, making him a Certified Professional of the Institute Professionnel des Comptables et Fiscalistes Agréés (IPCF). As a registered member of the institute, he has been running his own corporate consulting firm in Brussels to date.

Extracurricular activity: He studied French Language & Literature at the Université Libre de Bruxelles (ULB) for a few non-consecutive years (1985-87). In 1991, he participated in a summer course in Japanese Management at Sophia University in Tokyo. In 1999, he completed a semester-long Economics and Commerce programme, focusing on Business Law at the University of Sydney, Australia.

He was enthusiastically involved in cultural and sportive activities during his school days. He was such a fan of cricket that he took the game from the capital to the villages of Dohar in southern Dhaka (the home of his maternal grandparents), at a time when cricket was not played much in cities except Dhaka in East Pakistan at the time.

Shaupaun has been living abroad since 1977. He is very keen to know different cultures and people; he has travelled extensively to many parts of the world. In 2006, he created a voluntary organisation 'PraubashBaungau a.s.b.l.' based in Brussels.

Mr. Koumar and his wife, Rokshana (Rani), have two sons and a daughter, Aupourbau, Aushim and Shaurnally, and have maintained a permanent home in Brussels.

# Preface

This book *Naturocracy* is the result of self-discussions about nature, religion, society, and politics. I have been reminiscing about this quite a lot as memories of my motherland fill me with nostalgia — its fertile soil teeming with plants on which I crawled; the gurgling rivers whose waters I drank and where I used to fish and swim; the melodious songs of moonlight nights which lulled me to sleep.

The highly fertile land I had left behind was being destroyed mindlessly. The River Buriganga — once the lifeline of old Dhaka where I was born and where I had once lived — has now become the most polluted river-turned-drain in the capital city.

Thoughts stirred in my mind, but I was unable to express them. One day I took up my pen to write all my emotions. Since then I have been writing these pages day after day and little by little.

In the beginning, I started penning them in English and Bengali simultaneously. I avidly continued with a passionate amalgam of thinking, living, and writing processes. Time is life. As the years went on, I felt like I had fallen into the ocean; I reluctantly stopped writing the rest of its Bengali chapters. Along with some unexpected unbearable situations on the pathway of life, I lost hope and thought that I would not be able to finish the book. To be honest, I eventually abandoned every process; however, it never vanished from my mind — floating in vividly and ceaselessly.

In the end, I finished the book, reflecting on my vision of my motherland for posterity. I have dreams and aspirations; I heartily wish to see my country as a home where people of all colours and creeds live together in peace and happiness.

Brussels, January 20, 2009

Shaupaun Koumar

Chapter 1

# What Makes Me Think about all These?

## 1. Introduction

### 1.1 The laissez-faire economy works against the natural economy.

The livelihoods of the very ordinary people and a large part of the naturally rich land, waterways, ecosystems, and tropical rainforests have already been destroyed.

Bangladesh was once famously known as the land of marvellous rivers. A vast number of its traditional economic and social activities depended on those ecological livelihoods and natural waterways and drainage systems, which are now being extensively polluted and looted.

The whole society is, in fact, being contaminated by falsifications and dishonesty in the name of a religious majority. Paradoxically, only in this regard, all our major political parties are on the same steamboat and waving the same banner; otherwise, they are bitter enemies of each other.

It is imperative to learn now from the First World about the problems. We should examine these issues in terms of the environment holistically and carefully so that we do not encounter similar problems in the way of our development process. And then we must define feasible solutions for ecologically sustainable well-being so that future generations can enjoy their lives equally on the same earth as ours. First creating problems after problems for ourselves and then solving them is extremely difficult and mostly impossible.

Until a few decades ago, the rich imported raw materials from the poor and produced garments in their country. Now they have given that job to the poor and are getting finished clothes in return.

As a result, many poor people are becoming rich but at what cost to the environment? Toxic waste from the manufacturing industry is dumped in rivers and fields; the water that people drink has now become deadly poisonous; the soil has lost its fertility and is unable to support plantations. The true value of this is invaluable, intolerable, and irreplaceable.

If the rich put their problems on the poor, the poor will not see them until they become rich. We throw each other's toxic diseases into our mother earth and it bears all costs. So, we are so glad to have such a free container. But when nature ultimately and drastically takes its own course, who will suffer then?

Pollution has become a universal chronic disease; it travels everywhere regardless of those who pollute and those who do not. Since the start of the Industrial Revolution, people have become materially much richer but mentally quite poor. The rich are polluting despite dire warnings about environmental disasters. But under the guise of the Earth Summit, their powerful governments are continually cheating the people.

Once some natural (undeveloped) countries moved a proposal to protect the natural environment from devastating pollution. The rich disregarded it completely and were making fun of it: Ha … a summit of the poor!

But when this issue was strongly supported by environmental groups from all over the globe, then the most powerful polluters declared that they would put it in a process i.e., the environmental issue is put in a pipeline from which you cannot see its end.

In the meantime, developed countries have sold their obsolete techno-products to the poor. The wealthy now attend the summit from time to time only to derail its agenda. And their powerful media broadcast that the poor are using old cars and technologies and that they are the polluters of the world. This is their new game theory; it is pretty nearly like the Middle East Peace Process that has been there for ages, but so far not a single 'P' has ever come out of it.

Through the entire development process of human societies, while no wealthy nation existed, people would exchange natural goods and knowledge for their essential needs; this was a relationship of humanity.

Primitive industries depended heavily on manpower. Strong black Africans were bought as if they were beasts. And they would have been turned forever into Negro slaves by western whites. They would have been dragged by ropes to the sailboat that was heading for America. This was just cowboy culture to enslave children of God.

A poor man in the 20th century said, "Earth provides enough to satisfy every man's needs, but not every man's greed."

With a few wad of notes can be bought a forest including aboriginal people and other creatures without any hassle. The currency note has enormous buying power. However, you cannot eat money as food. If there is no food but lots of money, only then will you understand the value of nature.

If a poor country starts making weapons to become rich, the bourgeoisie mock by saying why it makes arms when it cannot feed its people. Tragedy is, that they sell weapons to the poor.

Tribal people live in a group. Each group has its own leader within a small territory; they know each other and always live together with their joy and sorrow day and night. Their language, culture, lifestyle, homes, and social status are all very much alike. Each problem they create and solve is done instantly. Naturally, they fight against each other. No matter how cruel a man or his entourage, how many people will they be able to kill, or how many things will they be able to destroy without weapons?

There is no doubt that technology brings more and more comfort, but it destroys happiness. It invites endless competition among humans — from their families to nations and everywhere around the globe. Without technology, their level of envy is very little. There is less competition, less anxiety, less jealousy … and much less mental illness.

Techno-product is non-essential. But it has tremendous power to dominate others. So, there is an exponential and overwhelming demand for it at any cost. Advancements in technology have, therefore, created the myriad problems of modern life.

Take a simple example, a handmade natural bag, wherever you throw it on the ground, is automatically treated by nature by turning it into fertile soil. People must have been amazed when it was first invented, which made their daily life easier. Nowadays, a plastic bag has made their modern life more comfortable; it is so cheap, so light, and extremely easy to carry; not only the poor, but the rich also abundantly use it. Governments collect taxes on it to live. Furthermore, it helps them pull up their GDP. Techno-products are largely government and bourgeois-friendly. Naturo-products, on the other hand, are friendly to the earth and the common people.

The rich do not throw away their plastic bags here and there; they have created a mechanism to collect those bags, which has created new jobs and further economic growth. But where do they eventually dump their techno-waste?

The poor throw away their plastic bags whenever and wherever they want. Plastics are everywhere. Food is contaminated with eye-catching plastic. Although plastic is inexpensive, it is abundantly costly for soil, water and health, — which are most essential for the survival of all living beings. This manmade environmental disease spreads everywhere without distinguishing between the poor and the rich.

It was in the 1970s, if I recall correctly, that there was a piece of news about Greenpeace. It was protesting against nuclear weapon tests and dumping toxic waste into the Pacific Ocean. The protesters were brutally assaulted by the naval forces. This told me then that the people of some developed countries had already realised the catastrophic environmental degradation caused by industrial activities. Their governments, nevertheless, went against their own people who understood the global problem.

The technocratic bourgeoisie think they have inherited the earth from their God, but the environmentalists know that they have borrowed it from their children.

You know their constant opportunism. Once they got a taste of colonialism, never did they want to give up its lure. Those whose only intention is to divide and rule can never be partners in peace in this world. No one can make peace because it always exists, but one can obviously destroy it.

Only if you realise that your knowledge is limited somewhere, will you understand the essence of knowledge. Someone may have discovered something, and it might have been proven by others. So, you can believe it; still, you have to rediscover it so that you yourself can understand it, which will give vitality to your understanding. Overall, realising its long-term adverse effects on the environment and health is still unknown to the inventors. You need to see each issue holistically to solve the problem locally.

A beast knows what their needs are; man knows what his greed is. Even if a man were ever able to create another human being, would it solve his problem?

There are so many brilliant, amazing, and unthinkable things happening around you all the time in nature; but you are probably unaware of them because you are unconsciously occupied with yourself only. One day you may wake up from your sleep and realise that while counting the stars, you have lost the moon.

The meaning of life is to live your life rather than keep analysing how it was formed. Since birth, the only thing you are sure of in life is that you will die; but why do you worry about it? Is there any difference if you live for 10 years or 100 years? Once you are gone, will you ever be able to regret saying why you have died today instead of tomorrow?

For a long time, many social scientists and politicians have been shouting that they will eradicate poverty from the planet. But can, or will they? It seems to me now that it is an ongoing political slogan only. In fact, poverty is the creation of human societies; if there are no poor, there will be no rich either. Do you think this planet has become rich after the commencement of industrial activities?

Before you help the poor, you create a situation of hysteria so that the poor need your help. Many naturally wealthy nations in this world have been impoverished by long centuries of colonisation and exploitation. If we can refrain ourselves from being rich, this will perhaps be the best help for the poor. If we cannot do this, we should simply stop helping the poor so that they can help themselves. They are quite content with what they get for free from nature. They do not want to depend on our artificial society in exchange for their way of life.

The destruction of indigenous homes and the rainforests in the name of development and modernisation is a grave crime against nature. Indigenous peoples are the principal guardians of the flora and fauna. They are innocent, naïve, and environmentally friendly; they have recognised the wisdom of nature; they are the icons of our diversified cultures. They do not want to be modernised; they want nothing from our so-called civilised society. They never impose their ideology on us; never do they interfere in our affairs. Not only do we destroy their heavenly homes and resources, but we also instil our beliefs in them. They do not need us at all; nonetheless, we cannot survive without them.

The general population all over the planet, either rich or poor, do not want materialistic lives but do want to live in peace and harmony with the amalgam of their joy and sorrow.

If no one had invented TV, nobody would ever have cried for it. It is a cunning marketing device to increase consumption. When people consume less, the economy goes into recession; in a laissez-faire economy, people actually misuse natural resources for capitalist economic growth. But never do they realise that the more they interfere with nature, the more they will suffer for it.

The root of this kind of behaviour is the relentless desire for more pleasure and power at the expense of others.

We must respect and accept the nature of nature as we are not above its principles. Nature blossoms anew each time in full diversity, but it always remains original.

Rainforests are the natural laboratories of many modern scientists; these forests constitute their livelihood too. Before imposing your lifestyle on them, you, city-based academicians, should understand the enormous values of indigenous knowledge and tradition. Many literate people often say that illiterate people are stupid, unfortunately, they do not understand that they themselves are ill-educated. Farmers work in the fields from childhood to death and accumulate a great deal of knowledge throughout their lives owing to their contact with nature, but never do they receive any degree for their invaluable wisdom.

Fewer and fewer people in industrialised nations actually know where their food comes from. In a city, people are very familiar with all modern facilities, but they hardly know who lives next door. They face a variety of social and mental disorders. All sorts of extreme crimes can be seen in the cities.

Though life in a village is difficult, its people rarely see such problems; they are much happier. If you compare any town and village either in the First or Third World, you will find similar differences between a town and a village. Squalor and poverty persist behind the city's glittering façade. Despite all the modern comforts, why is real life in a city so miserable?

A city covered with bricks and concrete cannot feed its people without muddy villages, but villages do not need any cities to survive. Trees can well enjoy their lives without humans; but without trees, people will have to return to their lost paradise.

Once you have the picture in your mind's eye, you will easily be able to see who the real culprits are for damaging the planet. Under no circumstances must we work against nature (we cannot afford to anymore), but together with it.

Growing institutional injustices, crimes, lies, corruption, arms trafficking, the arrogance of militarily powerful élites, and going to wars for oil and soil are the root causes of human and non-human suffering worldwide. Honesty or morality no longer gets its due in human society. The erosion of human principles in this age of modernisation is a grave threat to its goodness. I wish we had a free world without political borders, but that may no longer be possible since we humans are becoming more dangerous and cunning than we used to be in ancient times.

## 1.2 Historically and geo-culturally, Bangladesh is part of one of the world's oldest and most influential civilisations.

As an independent Bengali nation, we possess our own Bengali language and its distinct cultural heritage. As a geographical identity, from a global perspective, we are a part of one of the oldest and most influential civilisations in the world. We cannot separate ourselves from the glory of our ancient heritage with very long familial and cultural roots. We share the same air, the same water, and the same soil; the Bay of Bengal along the Indian Ocean and the home of the Royal Bengal Tigers are also part of our historical identity.

The finest Bengali muslin of ancient times is part of the tradition and history of present-day Bangladesh. Weavers, while weaving traditionally, used to sing and listen to melodious and meaningful Indian music. The riverbanks of ancient Bengal, especially on the banks of the Ganges, were famous for muslin: the most delicate and lightest fabric the world had ever seen.

Muslin was the name of a legendary cloth made of hand-woven fabric from pure natural cotton which is now extinct. It originated in Dhakeshwari of the then united Bengal. Dacca (now spelt Dhaka, since the 1980s, to hear its correct articulation, Bengali spelling ঢাকা remains as it is) had been the finest producer of muslin. Cotton was first used by the ancient Indus Valley civilisation, while the art of weaving itself has been traced to much earlier times. Neighbouring Persian, Arabian and Chinese merchants were the earlier trading partners of the ancient Indians. During the Silk Road transmission, natural products travelled from Asia to Europe on horsebacks and donkeys.

Ancient India became proficient in making cotton textiles, which were exported to the Roman Empire; the trade expanded in the Middle Ages following the growth of the maritime *Silk Road* in the Indian Ocean. The elegant nawabi dresses of Mughal Emperors and their colourful 'Sangeet Mahal' (music halls) shone with the muslin of ancient Dhaka.

Towards the end of the fifteenth century, European pirates infiltrated India and were astonished to see not only the quality and volume of cotton textiles in India but also its far-flung trade. While the smell of fine Indian cuisine from their neighbours reached England, the English pirates pushed their sailing boats into the sea to discover India — which had long been unknown to them.

They destroyed our muslin. They wanted to sell their cotton goods that were not comparable at all with ours. The John's Company's British pirate-turned-spice traders systematically rounded up the weavers and cut off their thumbs so that they could no longer make the muslin that had been amazing the world for centuries. Weavers fled their villages, changed occupations and starved to death due to famine that was deliberately created by ruining their artisanal lives — the death of indigenous knowledge.

When the *John Company* (later the East India Company) got free trading benefits owing to the generosity of the Mughal Emperors, those English pirates gradually seized power and used weapons against innocent people who never knew what guns ldooked like.

In order to suppress Hindu-Muslim unity, the British occupiers divided Bengal into West Bengal and East Bengal. They eventually divided India for the Muslim minority, without the consent of the people, which gave birth to Pakistan in 1947. Dacca (Dhaka) became the provincial capital of East Bengal of the new State (Pakistan), which — until 1971 — consisted of two parts, geographically separated by more than 1,800 kilometres. India remains in between with her two kids: one is to her right, and the other is to her left.

Eight years later, in 1955, the Urdu-loving Bengali Muslim leaders changed the name of East Bengal to East Pakistan. They did this even after the historic Bengali language movement in 1952, while the ordinary people went against those religious leaders for imposing Urdu as the only state language of Pakistan.

It is a matter of great regret that after breaking away from ex-Pakistan, we are yet to establish the full use of Bengali language in the bureaucratic systems. Muslim leaders in Bangladesh can no longer love Urdu freely, so they now love English. When they were Indians, they forbade Muslims from learning English and Bengali because these were not Islamic languages. On the other hand, on the eve of February 21 every year, they go to the Shaheed Minar and pretend that they are Bengalis.

The population of East Bengal was the majority compared to the total population of the other four provinces of Pakistan. That is to say, the Bengali-speaking population of the whole of Pakistan was in the majority, but our minority Muslim brothers forced the majority of our Muslim sisters to speak in Urdu. Moreover, Urdu is not the spoken language of any province of Pakistan. Interestingly, all our Bengali Muslim leaders in the National Assembly of Pakistan (1948) supported this unjust act of Jinnah-led Muslim leaders. What can be said about these religious brokers in the name of religious love?

Beware of them always! They invented an invisible product called 'religion' to make their living in this visible world. If they truly believe in the Almighty God, can they ever deceive people?

Before the partition of India, they were paid agents of English gunmen. Those gunmen made many unjust laws, which gave many privileges to local agents who worked for the occupiers at the expense of their own people. The generation of those mirjafarians (traitors) is always active in Bangladesh, but in different forms.

The English left, but their trained agents did not. Right after the bloodiest Partition (1947) in the history of the world, those agents took off their master's uniforms and disappeared into the crowd. So, it is not easy to identify them because they were the same people in this country and lived in the same place that took three different names (India, Pakistan, and Bangladesh) in three different political eras of the country's history. We need to watch carefully what Urdu-loving Bengalis are doing in Bangladesh, wearing their religious masks after their separation from Pakistan.

There will always be quarrels, disagreements, and different opinions among people. This is equally true of a family, but it does not allow anyone to deny one's original cultural and familial roots. The utter pride of many of our religious pundits often indicates that Bangladesh is the world, and we have come down from the 1971 sky.

None of our neighbours are Muslim countries. If we give up our true cultural identity, we will merely be strangers in the vicinity and the world arena. Even though most of our ancestors converted to Islam, we cannot be Arabs in any way, nor will they accept us as their people.

Before the creation of Pakistan, India was our country. But we detested India because we preferred the Muslim identity to the country's identity. When we partitioned India and became Pakistani Muslims, we still hated Hindu India; thereafter, we divorced our fellow Muslims; and we now loathe Hindus more than ever; we only loved them so much during our freedom struggle. This reflects our religious characteristics, of which we are very proud. Do we ever feel ashamed of not being a grateful nation?

Neither India nor Pakistan is our enemy. We had differences and disputes, but in the past, we had been living together peacefully for a long time. Pakistanis are Muslims too; why do we hate them now? We should understand ourselves first before loathing others. Remember, Pakistanis were never our colonial or occupying forces; we were born together from our ancestors — India. We have a long familial and cultural heritage. Our cultural diversity on the soil of the Indian subcontinent is so widespread and the family roots are so deep that we will never be able to root this out altogether. Our real enemies are those who never want to have good relations with our neighbouring countries.

We should deeply realise and remember that while the diverse people of India were living in natural and spiritual peace, British pirate-turned-spice traders smuggled arms into India to terrorise the masses. This ruined the peace of those nice days.

Chapter 2

# What Makes People Religious?

## 2.1 No one can be a worse sinner than those who are blatant liars and deceivers, and still shout for their religion and take pride in it.

The memories of freedom fighters were still very fresh in my mind when I left Bangladesh in 1977 as I was offered a job in Libya just after I graduated from the Marine Fisheries Academy. I had always hoped that my motherland would stand firm on its principles of the liberation war for which a free Bangladesh was born.

But since then, regrettably enough, I have been witnessing that this glorious spirit of our patriotic people has systematically been distorted not only by those who were against the principles of our freedom but also by those who really fought for it. Then what did we fight for? Was it just to deceive ordinary people?

Religion has been politically used to divide people. The British colonial power had used the policies of divide and rule to oppress and repress our people and country. Our policies must not be so deceitful and destructive.

How can a country be religious? Neither can it move, nor can it pray. Religion is believed to be a divine affair; can a state be a proxy of divinity?

Still — even if Islam is the religion of the state, all the citizens of Bangladesh should be followers of Islam. And the state must be governed by the authentic principles of the Quran; any amendment to it must be justified from its origin. And if the people do not obey the fundamental principles of the state religion, then they must be punished accordingly.

The government cannot play a twin role; on the one hand, calling Islam the only state religion in the constitution, and on the other hand, saying other religions may be practised in it. Then, should the state disobey its own religion by practising other religions?

If the state is really honest regarding other religions, then it must bear the names of other religions as state religions too.

It was the former Pakistan that was created as an Islamic state without the consent of its people; consequently, 24 years later, the common people in its eastern part wholeheartedly rejected such an idea; thus a free-thinking Bangladesh was born as a secular state as per its constitution.

A religious name does not make a person religious; a virtuous person is religious even if he or she does not possess any name.

Bangladesh has become the most corrupt country in the world, and it continues to maintain this unfortunate distinction even after so many years. This is even more disgraceful for a country associated with Islam.

As 90% or so of the population of the country is Muslim, then what is the meaning of being religious if we are dishonest?

Imams under their leadership make us pray, but never do they do the same to be truthful. They perhaps think that Allah sees only their prayers but not their sins. If they truly believe that the Almighty sees everything, then could they commit any sin behind their religious attire? In a dealing, they often suggest, pointing to someone, that you can definitely trust him for anything because he prays five times a day. Is it a valid argument?

If a person wearing religious fashion indulges in venality, people hardly say anything against them; but if the same person without it commits the same misconduct, people react instantly. Why do they judge someone's religiousness based on their fashion rather than actions? Does a person's religiosity reassure them that the person is honest?

Will an evil person ever cheat people by wearing the uniform of a devil, or will he do so by wearing the uniform of a religious man?

If you do whatever you like in the name of religion, it is not a sin in our society; you are always honoured to preach the messages of the merciful Allah. But if you follow the path of truthfulness and criticise the dishonesty of god-fearing people without a religious flag, you will become enemies of Allah. The lovers of Allah will march against you in the streets like a flock of sheep. Our society believes that religious scholars are impeccable people and that no matter what they do or wherever they enter, every unholy thing becomes sacred.

If a religious institute is corrupt, how can people have faith in it? If you practise your religion for nefarious purposes, do you not deceive the Almighty?

Corruption is a chronic social disease and has become an open competition between people from almost every section of the country. The life of true honest persons is getting much harder day by day. Unscrupulous people gang up to make honest people dishonest by carrying out sly tricks in order to freely fulfil their greed.

Before, people were afraid of indulging in corruption. Now, the corrupt have a loud voice. Interestingly, they dictate religious affairs. But never can they say that unscrupulousness is a good thing. Because their conscience rejects it, but their religion does not, which is why they are corrupt. If a religious institution is immoral and corrupt, then what does their religion and divinity mean to them?

Is religion for a deity or communalism?

Nobody says: "I believe in the sun." Because there is no reason not to believe in it. It is where it is. The truth is truth.

If adherents of all religions have love for the truth, then all human beings separately belong to the same religion — the religion of truthfulness; in this regard, there is no division among us. Still, where is the division?

When we talk about one's belief, there is a question of doubt; but this does not mean that one's faith is untrue; suspecting anything merely implies that something needs to be examined. The outcomes can be either true or false, of course, if the answer to the question is within our knowledge; otherwise, faith remains as it is.

But difficulties arise when someone indoctrinates others with their faith. If you are a truth-loving person, you can discuss and research your personal beliefs; however, you have no right to impose your own dogma on others. If you still do, there is an obvious problem in your beliefs; either you do not want the ultimate truth ever to be disclosed, or you want to establish your own supremacy over others with your ignorance.

Why are we Islamists so dead against other believers? What is the difference between those who believe that God exists, and those who believe that he does not exist? Are they not the same since they both rely on their own beliefs?

Any man could say that a fairy comes to see him every night; can you believe it even if you cannot prove that it does not exist?

"I believe in ghosts," she says.

"I do not believe in ghosts," someone else answers.

The believer cannot claim that the unbeliever is a believer of 'no-ghost'. Before preaching their faith in ghosts, ghost believers have to prove how they came to know of their existence.

If a blind person tells you that you must not open your eyes or else god will punish you, must you keep your eyes closed for fear of god?

What is our problem if someone says that she does not believe in the existence of air?

Shall we go to kill her in the dark, saying that she is an infidel?

If you apply your innate knowledge, you can make her feel that air exists in her body as well. The dharma of air is that it occupies space and has enormous power that can be realised when the wind blows violently. If you do not have that kind of knowledge, just ignore what she says about air.

Do we think that if we abhor other humans' faith, we will all get free tickets to reach heaven? Were other believers created by a different Allah?

Why are we Bengali Muslims always blindly and madly against Hindus and Buddhists? Are we fearful of recalling the root of our historical evolution?

If religion could make someone honest, then all religious people would have a good heart, but unfortunately, that is not the case. The character or dharma of every human being is unique, which must not be communal. Religion can have no value for humankind unless its devotees can show its goodness. Goodness or badness is the individual property of a person. Going against other believers believing that you will be rewarded by god in the eternal world is sheer nonsense.

If religion is given by god, he knows very well who is religious and who is not; it is not a man's job to judge it. But why are they the guardians of god's religion? Doesn't the almighty have the power to protect it?

Religion is not a show business for human society; it is not a commodity for sale, nor is it a question of fear or greed. Religious beliefs should be practised privately in peace and harmony for your own satisfaction. If you can build a house to rent, you can definitely set aside a place in the house for such practice.

If you are truly religious, i.e., religion is not imposed upon you, but you believe in it based on your own wisdom, then you should know that each one of us is entirely and solely responsible for our own beliefs, actions, and intentions; no one is accountable for someone else's religious affairs.

But why do Imams call us every time and even make us join them for prayers? Why are they so desperate to take us to their paradise? Are they sure themselves that they will go to heaven?

Why don't they punish sinners rather than obliging them to ask for forgiveness?

While I was a child, I used to go to a madrasah early in the morning for religious studies under Tootha Mawlana. He was also my primary school teacher. He seldom used to attend any religious rituals, but when he did, he never took money or any other benefit for this. He was very critical of this practice. For this reason, the local clerics forbade him to attend their religious discourse (owas mahafil).

It was at that time that my mind stirred with many questions about religion and the creator (beedhata). But the theory of our religion is to believe without arguing, that's all! Now, I tell myself that if this is the theology of faith, then anyone can say something and demand that mankind must believe in it. Should they?

During my childhood, I used to take part in religious discourses, where I observed that no person was allowed, nor did anyone dare to question the preacher's speech. Undoubtedly, I could not ask any questions that came to mind while listening to the discourse. A child has no right to raise any question about his or her religion, but they have an obligation to believe.

It is a great pity that even people like Tootha Mawlana are ill-treated by fanatics, and not by virtuous people. These self-proclaimed protectors of religion always make new dogmas in the name of Allah. Traditional people who dominate society salute them and go against people like Tootha Mawlana.

A human has no control over his or her own mind, but over one's tongue. Hence, one can say whatever one wants, but the mind knows the truth. You cannot escape your mind even if you hide in the dark.

Most of our early beliefs stem from our parents. I have been brought up in the Muslim tradition of the Indian subcontinent; as far as I can, it is my gratification to inquire about its roots.

To heed a cry for help is not a legal duty but a moral one. Piety and morality are two different things: a pious man can be immoral, and an impious man can be moral.

If you look beyond prehistoric times, you can easily see that primitive people of different geographical regions of that period worshipped natural phenomena such as thunderstorms, rain, fire, flood, high tide, low tide, moon, and sun — which mesmerised their minds; these were always essential for all beings. Without any theologian, that was their earnest respect for this mysterious universe.

But no human being knows who their creator(s) is — whether it is an object or insect, a male or female, singular or plural, i.e., nobody has ever been capable of understanding the creator (beedhata) of the universe.

The people of our primitive society had a good sense of natural phenomena as they worshipped the sun god, the moon god, the fire god ... instead of a marionette god. The early primitive people were free from any formal religion and government; there was no money to be exchanged and to buy something or somebody. They worshipped whatever impressed them. They did so of their own free-will in the absence of any house of deity — whenever and wherever they wanted.

When we try to understand what Deity is, our first problem is that we cannot see him. Therefore, when it comes to the question of the creator, only our personal beliefs and non-beliefs always coincide. But in the question of religious organisations, human involvement is palpably seen. Thus, in this regard, one must be very careful in linking someone's religious beliefs with the creator of this universe. Human beings are a tiny part of nature, nothing else.

Many people understand God very easily and instantly say, "look at all this, nothing could have existed without a creator."

I always wonder whether they have ever realised that this statement is self-contradictory.

If there are mistakes and misrepresentations in someone's book, someone else can correct or clarify them but can he do such a thing in the book of god? Since god has given his holy book to mankind, they need to read it. If they are confused, the deity can clarify the matter. But why do clerics do this? How do they know what he meant to say about the conflicting statements in the holy book?

It is also seen in the courts of Bangladesh that non-Muslims are not allowed to touch the Quran. If Allah has given the Quran to all mankind, how will they accept it as the sacred book of humanity without touching and reading it first?

Religion is something in which people have blind faith — maybe because the creator is linked with it; evil persons, in a religious style, take this as an absolute opportunity for their personal gains. In fact, religion is the best tool in this world to control and command senseless people.

Being a member of a religious organisation does not necessarily mean that the person is virtuous. The name of an institute itself does nothing; neither does it move, nor does it act. It is all about the work of its individual members. If truthfulness or virtuousness is a fundamental principle of religion, can an impious person belong to it?

While religion is the most difficult and spiritual theme for any adult, how can a baby be baptised in the name of religion? Teaching a child about religion and certifying a child as a believer by a religious institution is not the same thing.

The law and order of a country are not to represent the divine order, but rather it is to manage undisciplined human societies in relation to their social evolution and behaviour. If the creator had ever given a holy book to a man to rule the earth, he could easily have given a true copy of it directly to every human being. Nature is a great example for each one of us; no one gets anything clandestinely from nature.

Has the existing constitution of Bangladesh become divine after adding 'Bismillah' to it? Is that not intended to fool the public? And who are the fools — Islamic scholars, or their followers?

No Muslim woman can accept or be at the helm of a country because there is no female leadership in Islam. What kind of Islam was then introduced in Bangladesh, where women were leading Islamic men? Are they Muslims in their name or by faith?

Does the Ministry of Religion consult its divinity before giving any religious instructions to the people?

The righteous path, with the spiritual mind but without credos, is very natural and easy. To tell the truth, you do not have to do anything, just say what you see. But in order to lie, you have to invent a method of falsification against the truth. If you do not use your inborn knowledge wisely, but go against the truth by following the orders of your religious masters, do you not act against the creator by denying the truth?

I do not think God has given a trade licence to any preachers for lying in the name of divinity.

If we do not understand the creator, it does not matter at all — because it is unthinkable to just perceive the universe. But if you intentionally lie in favour of your religion, it is crystal clear that you do believe in true sinners rather than a true god.

To be a truly religious person you have to do nothing; just have a free mind without any attachment to reject lies and appreciate the truth.

Religion is a form of worship based on the faiths of various sects of human beings. The equivalent word used in Bengali for religion is dharma (Sanskrit), but the word essentially means the natural quality or behaviour of any being. For instance, the dharma of water, fire or a person is quite different. The dharma of a person — not one's religion — tells us what his or her nature is. The karma of a person needs to be judged, not his or her religion. Goodness is an act of dignity of an individual, which in itself is true religion; the name of its actor is the identity of a person, not of an institution. An institution is the name of a group of individuals, which does nothing.

Thinking is something that each human being does naturally. People cannot think collectively; even for the same thing, each person thinks independently and differently. The results of each thought can be shared with others, but thinking is an autonomous process. While I eat something, I do not think that it reduces the hunger of another. Similarly, one cannot sleep for others.

Religion is the same for me. It is not a table that you need helpers to take it to heaven.

## 2.2 What does it mean when bigoted religio-politicians say that someone has hurt their religious sentiments? Doesn't corruption in religion hurt religious sentiments?

If we kill people, loot their valuables, and grab their terrains by saying that they have hurt our religious sentiments — by committing such crimes — then do we not invite other believers to do the same to us? If this is the teaching of religion, it has to be uprooted from the planet. It cannot be the religion of God; it can only be the religion of serial killers.

Don't those who eat pork hurt the religious sentiments of Muslims? Will you murder them to establish the will of Allah?

What about women who do not don burkas? Singers, musicians, film stars … are they Muslims? Do their actions not hurt the religious sentiments of the majority in the country?

Shia, Sunni, Ahmadi … are they all the same? Does a religious sect not hurt the religious sentiments of another sect? And are they not infidels in each other's eyes?

Every day a little innocent flower is raped and killed, and then her body is thrown in a garbage bin by our Muslim brothers in present-day Bangladesh. No person in any Muslim political organisation, mosque or madrasah has butchered these criminals and looted them or grabbed lands. Are these Muslim rapists not hurting the Muslim religious sentiments? Or is this allowed in Islam? Will Allah ever forgive them if they worship him?

Can Muslims do whatever they want by saying Bismillah, and then everything can be halal?

Religio-politicians often say that terrorists have no religion. In fact, it is a political mantra for their followers as they do nothing about these deadly criminals. If their holy book says to kill infidels, then it is quite clear that these terrorists have a religion as they execute their religious duty by murdering others. So, instead of saying that terrorists have no religion, they should confess that killing the infidel is authorised in their religion; therefore, they merely do their religious duty in this way.

But why can they not admit this straight away? Because their conscience does not agree with the words of their holy book.

Islam is only the name of a religious organisation; it has no merit or demerit in its character. If its followers worked for world peace, it would be a religion of peace; if they did the contrary, it would be considered a religion of anti-peace.

A good act of an individual disciple promotes the goodness of a religion; likewise, his or her bad act intensifies the badness of that religion.

Religion is not a corporate commodity that can be bought and sold in the name of God. This abstract name is used on every occasion by religious traders just to deceive people easily; they would not believe them otherwise.

For centuries, corrupt politicians have been giving religious merchants all kinds of privileges; thus, the core principle of humanity is greatly declining in the world.

If the superstition of a community can be enforced as the religion of god in society — and if people question its authenticity before they believe it, can it hurt religious sentiments? Those who indoctrinate their prejudices in the minds of others must answer this question instead of accusing others of hurting their religion.

One might believe that a banana tree is God. This certainly cannot be a problem for others, and they should be tolerant of this if they are humane. However, if that person preaches to believe in it, they can say whatever they think about the banana god. But can it hurt the religious sentiments of banana lovers?

On the other hand, it is super difficult to believe and identify the invisible God. Angels and Satan are also not visible, and it is absolutely impossible to distinguish between them.

## 2.3 Have you sold your conscience to religion?

Many irreligious and immoral acts are often committed in religious institutions, but their disciples never destroy those unethical organisations. Instead, they collaboratively hide their wilful sins. Yet, they enter the same holy place again — wearing a fresh holy dress — to earn halal bread and butter.

If you talk about the evil acts of religious leaders, they will do nothing about this; on the contrary, they will attack you by saying that you have hurt their religious sentiments. And all fanatics will follow them as they are the majority.

Democracy belongs to mobocracy; mobocracy belongs to the conspiracy.

If you say, "I have raised questions about their irreligious deeds in the religious institution." Nobody will even listen to you because you have no value as a person without a religious appearance. The media will rarely notice you because they belong to the same élite community.

Sometimes an élite group tries to show their ethics towards journalism by saying that some fanatics have attacked temples and houses of minority Hindus and looted their valuables. The media do not say which religion those attackers belong to; but when one bigot does something good, the media gushes by saying that he was a Muslim man.

Thus, the majority of the media, politicians, and we Muslims directly or indirectly nurture religious bigotry in our society. Therefore, the religious frenzy is rapidly growing and destroying the true religious values that once existed in our harmonious society.

As fanatics always get blind support from the majority, they probably do not think they are guilty of an organised crime; rather, they are the heroes. Thus, it is not mainly dogmatic, but we — the opportunistic majority — are primarily responsible for this catastrophic situation in our society.

People are now very confused by the manipulated news of today's media revolutionary world; the media publishes anything by anyone and whatever is said, without any justification; if it sells some teashop gossip as news, what is the difference between them and the gossipy people? Irresponsible journalism undermines the morality of their professionalism.

A community defends their terrible crimes by saying that crime exists in other communities too. This only confirms their own crimes. And one crime in a country cannot be compared to hundreds of crimes in another country. Also, the nature and magnitude of crimes between the communities need to be judged.

Islamic fanatic theologians have spread throughout Bangladesh. They have taken over every corner of society like octopuses; many of them do not have common sense; they do not even know about the fundamentals and history of their own religion. How can they teach someone about something they do not know? Yet, what can be said about those students who admire such a teacher? Never can knowledge seep through a closed mind.

If an Imam lies and commits a sin, he must be punished before the locals, who will never let him enter the Mosque until he can show them that god has pardoned his sin.

But if he is not punished, shall you then go to pray therein again? Is that house of god still holy? Amazingly, these sinners issue fatwas against those who demand severe punishment for religious crooks.

The daily teachings of our ancestors were — do not lie; always stand up for innocent vulnerable people, whoever they are and whatever their religion is. And be against the aggressors and the looters if you can; otherwise, at least hate them.

## 2.4 If religion is given by God, why do humans rule it?

Religious preachers use almost every product made by infidels. They see human technology every day but do not understand how it was made. However, they do comprehend everything about god — what he thinks, and what floor of the sky he sleeps on.

Imams teach us how long and short our clothes must be; whereas during the Stone Age, people lived in the nude for millennia before the birth of a religious guru. Have those people gone to hell for not wearing religiously coded clothes?

In prehistoric times, no religious leader had descended from heaven to make a piece of cloth for them. But when the cunning men saw that someone else had made their clothes, they quickly understood the potential light of civilisation and learned how to dress. Soon after, they inaugurated a religious dress code and promoted themselves to the upper classes of human society by creating division of labour. Since then they no longer have to go hunting for their own food; the prey comes up to their decorated table as delicious food.

The pioneering religio-economists very slyly inaugurated an everlasting business in the name of religion, which required no capital. In a religious economy, there is no risk of inflation, deflation, and bankruptcy. Their income is tax-free, audit-free, and everything else-free.

They realised that most people in the world are like flocks of sheep, so their marketing strategy was to target that bunch of people. These nature-loving naïve people were very honest and pacifist; they worshipped the sun, moon, fire, river, etc., for which they could freely enjoy their livelihood, and all this was free. In order to make them lifelong blind disciples of religion, those wily religio-economists made only two types of life-supporting pills, God and Religion, without using any element or raw materials of natural economies.

At a very early stage, they declared themselves to be the gods of their respective tribal peoples. In the Dark Ages, they did not know how big the earth was, but they told those naïve people some imaginary tales about its creation. In light of their untrustworthy activities, people no longer trusted their religious gods. Then they said that the deities were invisible and living in heaven.

As human civilisation evolved, a biblical theologian claimed that, in fact, there was only one god. And he sends messages to the people of the world through his agents. He was defined as formless, eternal, and omnipotent.

An amorphous thing, if any, would be an object. But why is it called ‘he’? In some verses of the Quran, the pronoun ‘we’ has been used when Allah is the speaker. In no circumstances, however, will one ever be able to deny the existence of such a fantastic god — one that can only be sold and bought in religious shops.

Thus, the last self-appointed preachers had only one thing to do; i.e., to get as many clients as possible for their organisation by any means, be it fear or by luring.

So, they tell their disciples that go everywhere with the nomads, make all people believers of our only true religion, and force them to worship God through our priests to secure a better place in heaven. And kill all those who are infidels. Only those who follow our religion will go to paradise; everyone else will get a red ticket to go to hell.

However, if anyone disobeys god’s commandments, we will punish them accordingly. But remember, our god is so merciful; if you pray to him, he will absolve you of all your sins. Hence, for his sake, we will make sacred places everywhere on earth. If you give us a penny, you will get a million from him; please give us what you can for the house of god. Your money will not be worthless, and it will ensure your eternal life in paradise as well.

Nowadays, everywhere in Bangladesh, people are accustomed to hearing such incitement of temptations, where loud voices are used as a tool to beg in the name of Allah. Nowhere in the world, not even in the Arab world, is the name of Allah misused in this way.

But people are in a hurry to be overly generous to Allah; they throw coins and notes to buy the fortune of eternity. Not only adults, but infants are also given equal opportunity to purchase a share of their religious organisation; even newborn babies become their ardent disciples. The more temptation one religion offers, the more followers it gets.

Isn’t a hungry person who begs for the stomach much better than such religious beggars?

Clerics and Imams walk hand in hand on the streets of Bangladesh like the kings of paradise. The Almighty does not talk to ordinary people; he speaks only to the scholars of heaven, who interpret his messages for mankind.

Our society hates poor beggars but adores religious beggars. Religious commerce has become a booming industry and is absolutely secure. Since the mute god never reacted, tribal religious sects grew rapidly. And then they went to wars — for centuries, killing and killing — to establish someone's religious supremacy and to occupy the continents of other people in the world.

Slums are widespread in Bangladesh, especially in Dhaka and other major cities; unwanted and illegitimate childbirths are awful in that overcrowded filthy locality. Mainly the middle and upper classes control their birth rate spontaneously, but the birth rate in slum areas is increasing exponentially. These dramatically increasingly superstitious people ultimately lead the society and dictate religious affairs.

A slum begins to form mainly in the public domain and the unprotected lands of the country. At a certain time, some people with religious looks, surround a place with natural fibre and bamboo. In order to keep it permanent and safe, they quickly call it the house of Allah; and behind it, a residence for an Imam is secured first. No one knows or tries to find out whether the man has any knowledge of religion; only his religious appearance is enough to certify that he is so. Thereafter, he chalks out a schedule for each meal at different houses in the area. Many families cannot afford to eat a good meal in their daily life, but they have to make a good meal for the Imam.

When the place of worship and the residence of an Imam are secured, the expansion of the mosque begins with those who follow the Imam. They put up mikes on the side streets and constantly demand money from passers-by for the house of Allah. Finally, the house becomes a superb building for worshippers with many business shops in it. Countless amounts of money come from the streets, shops, and everywhere without any accountability.

When the authorities come to pull down the slums, seldom do they touch houses of worship, even though they were built illegally and immorally; the authorities may think that Allah will be angry with them. But will he not be angry if they do not do anything against these evildoers?

Entering these divine places, do people ever think honestly about whom they actually worship?

No one questions who is playing the role of Allah in this process. But this word has a magical power to make money for religious traders in Bangladesh.

Therefore, they are more and more encouraged to build a mosque in this way. Such a bunch of miscreants get a huge income from free permanent accommodation, free food, and business facilities in the mosque. Astonishingly, no religious institution has ever protested against such sinful establishments or taken any punitive action. How can they accept such sinners as followers of divinity? If these people can run a mosque, what does religion mean to them?

Still, you go there to pray and bow down to these Imams to reach heaven.

Many madrasahs and orphanages are being established likewise in the country; there are many orphanages out there — but where do these innumerable orphans come from? Many of them are being incredibly abused. No Imam comes to punish the abusers. But they often lash poor women with a cane for not obeying the orders of Allah. The Ministry of Religion only watches such scenes. The public says nothing because they are very scared of such horrible acts by the defenders of religion and because our religious belief is such that nothing happens without the orders and will of Allah. Consequently, there is a huge demand in our society to be religious in any fraudulent and coercive way. Everything is eternally safe for these holy men.

## 2.5 Democracy belongs to mobocracy; mobocracy belongs to the conspiracy.

As most people just follow the herd, it is much easier for religio-politicians to turn them into mobs. Every good, bad, fanatic, pious or wise person democratically possesses equal voting rights. If the bigots are the majority, they will always win an election; hence, pious persons will have to follow the principles of bigotry as the bigots are desperate to make a bigoted world.

A pious person may normally vote sensibly and not chase corrupt politicians but may not stand openly against the injustice done by the mob.

A deadly crook, on the other hand, can vote for a criminal and also be a fanatical force in favour of unscrupulous politicians.

An innocent person will not usually chase a judge because he or she expects that the culprit will be punished by law. But they are always desperate to avoid punishment through any deceit; they chase the lawyer, bribe the judge, and commit other crimes to save their criminal lives; if all their efforts go in vain, they eventually may kill the judge. It can be otherwise inferred that criminals are the main attractive clients for a lawyer as they are so frantic to defend themselves at all costs.

Democracy does not elect a person of quality or justice but of popularity. The partisan political system actually invites dishonest and violent people, which undermines the core values of a society. Even in the richest democracies, there are always lies and conflicts amongst the parties. Thus, never would there be any political solution anywhere in the human world.

To know the merit of a student, does a teacher ask for a vote in the class? If most people agree that the earth is flat because that is what the holy texts say, can it still be accepted? If all people believe this, what will be the consequences?

Those who lie purposefully and do not acknowledge the truth have to invent many lies for the same lie; at the end of the day, they cannot keep track of all the lies — but if they are able to get the majority on their side, their whole job is done.

If the majority can do whatever they want against the minority, what is wrong with a dictator? The dictatorship of 51% of the masses is far more dangerous than that of a single person. In olden times, many good kings ruled their kingdoms very well and did a good job of dispensing justice honestly. Nevertheless, there were bad kings too. The democratic system has created an opportunity for gangsters to come to power by intimidating society. The advantage for them is that even though they may commit misconduct, they can always claim that they are elected by the people.

The mob is a very poisonous element. They are the products of dishonest politicians and self-proclaimed religious leaders. For their nefarious designs, they do not like to have a peaceful community but love creating chaos and anarchy in society so that they can play a role behind closed doors.

Since most people of the world are naïve and not very determined, they can very easily be transformed into a mob through any conspiracy against democracy. Freedom of expression must not be the freedom to deliberately falsify. No one's freedom should hinder the freedom of others.

People talk about democracy, but they always follow their absolute autocratic religion. It is the sole dictator in our daily lives; even babies and children cannot escape this harsh dictatorship.

Family members are always first in social life. But why is a person of dynasty in politics often negatively criticised in elections without being judged for merit? Candidates should be judged on the basis of their personal qualifications and shortcomings rather than their familial or non-familial connections. If two candidates with the same qualifications and skills compete for leadership, the person whose family was or is on the throne usually possesses more knowledge than the other in this case.

But those who randomly speak against dynastic rulers, probably know they have no good qualities to display. Why do people want change, and why do they set a specific time period for it? A change is needed when crucial things are not going well; then an immediate change may prevent the problems from mounting further. But as long as a leader performs his or her duties in good faith and efficiently, he or she should be given more collective support to carry out his or her work smoothly in the interest of the general public.

Most people do not care who rules the country, but they do care about how well it is governed. Voters seldom get the chance to choose the best person available. If a dictator is a good and capable person, then the common people will be best served by that dictator. We should understand that a dictator does not rule a country without its people.

## 2.6 Who are the minority or majority among humans? Do dishonest people belong to the majority or minority group?

Men and women are two naturally distinct groups of humankind, but which group holds the majority?

Does one in the minority suffer less than the one in majority? If one person is killed here, and if ten persons are killed there in the same way, will the suffering of ten be ten times greater than that of one person?

The only difference here is the number of people, but the pain is the same for each of the 11 people. None of them has less pain than the others.

There are 100 inhabitants living in a country, 90 in A, 6 in B and the rest equally among C and D religious groups. The government has 100 sweet mangoes to distribute, so each of the citizens will receive one. In this case, you do not need to know who the majority or minority is.

If you consider all residents as individual citizens of the country, as you belong to nature, there is no conflict. In the above example, if you look at Group A, each of them has got a mango, and they all collectively have received the full 90% of their share.

Now, if Group D demands that since there are four groups, we should divide the resources into four parts so that each group gets 25 mangoes.

It is, indeed, an illogical claim in the logical sense; it can still be a legitimate claim legally. Logic is innate knowledge; legitimacy belongs to human texts.

So, if you give privilege to a particular religious group without any valid reason, there will always be conflicts and chaos unless you clearly define the function of each group with their holy books.

In this case, the demand for D can anger the people of Group A; they can tell D that, "you are only two people in your group and have got your 2% share; you cannot demand more than that."

If Group D replies that, "since in this case, you are speaking reasonably today, we will gladly agree to take two mangoes. But remember, if your majority group again imposes any undue dominance over our minorities, we will ask you to practise 90% of our beliefs in your daily life. All right?"

"What the hell are you talking about? How dare you insult our religion! You are in the minority; give us back the two mangoes you have and get out of here. The decision belongs to the majority."

Compassion and hatred do not come from any religion but someone's mind. If one believes in true religion, then each person has to navigate their mind towards the right path of his or her own choice. It cannot be communalised in any way.

## 2.7 What does it mean to constitutionally bind everyone under a particular religion by the state?

How do you calculate the majority and the minority? And how can you measure one's religiosity?

The Islamic sects — Sunni, Shia, Wahhabi, Ibadi and Ahmadi — all have different beliefs even though they worship the same god. What religion do they really follow? Do honest, dishonest, virtuous, and evil persons belong to the same religion? If so, are they all religious? If the answer is still 'yes', then what does religion mean?

The names of all religions and their respective authentic sacred books where devotees believe in their own consent, need to be known first to the Ministry of Religion. Second, adults must register their names with the organ of their own religious authority. Only then will it be easier for people to know who belongs to which faith. If a scholar sins, he must receive the maximum punishment.

Imams must have perfect knowledge of what they are teaching and the language they are using. There are many Islamic institutes in Bangladesh, but there is no chief leader to deal with their doctrines; why? Do they have the capacity to preach Islam?

Who directs Islamic affairs in the wider world without a recognised Islamic religious leader in the Arab world?

There are numerous Islamic political parties in Bangladesh; they all pompously claim that they represent 90% of the Muslim population. Ironically, none of them has ever been able to form a government in the country's history; even all Islamic parties have never been able to form their own government together. Because they themselves are enemies of each other, even though they are all spokespersons of Islam. However, they all become a bunch of terrifying religious forces against other religions. If there is no other religious minority left in the country, there will be no more unity amongst Islamic parties, then they will have nothing else to do except fight against their own sects. In the end, they would be fighting against themselves to reach heaven.

A religious institution must record its good and bad deeds equally and chronologically in order to judge the faith of its true devotees. If the institute takes pride in the good acts of its disciples, thereby displaying the name of their religion, then the names and religions of the perpetrators should also be displayed so that crime has no place in their religion.

Corruption in religious organisations (church, mosque, temple, etc.) is the most sinful crime that humanity can commit in the name of God. This is cheating on him. If a religious institute can be corrupt, then the government and the entire society can easily be corrupt. If people could speak honestly and openly against religious actors, corruption in non-religious organisations would surely diminish.

People are blind when it comes to their own religion because they have always heard about it since birth. This blind faith of the disciples is capitalised upon by evil-minded people who use religious institutes as their safe havens. That is why a chaotic Muslim-majority Bangladesh has seen a huge increase in fake religious lovers.

The media, whenever they want, enters the home of any poor family and flashes their private matters in public by converting them into attractive news headlines. Hardly does the media ever talk about corruption in religious institutions.

Allah is surely smiling and keeping our records that will be shown on doomsday and reveal what role we are playing in his name.

In any general discussion people always refer to the Quran so smartly as if they were the spokespersons of the Almighty, but many of them have never touched the holy book. Never should one underestimate the power of ignorance.

## 2.8 Why is it necessary to have a mike to announce every prayer time every day? If the system is really required, it can be done by God-given tongue, not by man-made mike.

Hardly do clerics come to help with any social work as they are always busy praying to take us to their paradise. But do you think this world is hell? Yes, that is why our divine man promised us that lots of beautiful fairies were eagerly waiting for us in heaven. So, we are not happy in this world in any way. Our religion tells us that we must not laugh, sing, and enjoy here because these are all sins; we must cry all the time for the Imam's blessings to reach paradise.

How will they serve people when they spend all their time in the prison of the prayer house? People are tamed by religious doctrines to deny them enjoying the bounties of nature.

Not so long ago (even still), a small stick of a plant was used to measure the sun's shadow to know the natural time of day; then no Imam could invent a mike to announce the time of worship. But when other people invented it, the Imams denounced this invention and forbade its use in their pronouncements. Later, in contrast, they are happily using the mike without feeling any shame about their religious dogmas. Their call for worship appears whenever they receive any instruction from paradise and they declare it to the public.

Imams always lecture us that if more and more Muslims worship together in a mosque, they will earn bonus points. If so, there should only be a mosque where all devotees can pray together to secure the best place in paradise. Why do they ask people to go to mosques to worship Allah? Has he appointed them to allocate a higher mark to us to go to paradise?

Their intention is questionable; they build a mosque, but why do they call it the house of Allah instead of the house of the Imams? Praying five times a day is an obligation for a Muslim but going to a mosque isn't.

Many of our educated people ignore illiterate people because they cannot read and write even if they can speak. But many educated Imams who teach us about heaven and say that Arabic is the language of Allah, cannot speak and understand Arabic; are they not worse off than illiterate people?

A mike is often purposefully used in Bangladesh to grab land and property of vulnerable people by corrupt religious leaders. They use a mosque in an ugly way, from which occasional emergency calls come out as if they have just received a special order from the divinity that says that someone has insulted their religion. And the ready-made mob immediately obey Allah's orders by burning people's houses and looting their valuables.

No Imam, who has true love for the deity, can support such a grave crime and pray again at that place of worship with bloody criminals and liars.

According to the Bible and Quran, the first human disobeyed the order of God by eating the forbidden fruit for which Adam was thrown out of heaven as his punishment. Ironically, the same Deity is now incapable of doing anything against these blatant sinners.

Noise pollution in Dhaka city is the worst in the world; a mike is its main and constant source. An Imam uses a mike as a rival to other mosques that are located just nearby. They force others not to talk during the announcement, but they themselves are constantly making loud noises. They do not have compassion for others, but they compel others to have compassion for them. This is their principle as religious guards. They oblige the poor and hardship-stricken workers to stop working during the azan (announcement of prayer time). Their religious duty does not allow even a sick person to sleep soundly.

If they cannot sleep at night because of the heavy burden of their sins, they can ask for God's forgiveness in their holy house; however, they should not think that others are like them.

Can the creator say that prayer is better than sleep?

Why don't the Imams announce our eating time of the day and sleeping time of the night? These are two fundamental obligations given by nature without which everybody will perish.

If you are truly religious, above all, mustn't you know your prayer time? Why do you depend on Imams for this?

Even on a dark cloudy day, a bird knows when it is morning and when it is evening — their time to eat and their time to sleep. Imams need to learn from beasts about natural times and a great deal of other things too.

Clerics with the title of Hazrat Mawlana talk about religion like reciting a poem. They hang mikes not only in their lecture hall but also outside the place and in front of the houses in the vicinity to compel others to listen. They start giving speeches without restrictions at any time of the day and night. They speak so fast and quote the word of Allah in a way that sounds as if they were present in heaven listening to the Almighty.

They do not allow the audience to ask any questions or discuss their monologue. Nobody even asks if they have the knowledge to talk about world history and divinity. But the worshippers swallow their speeches with so much gratitude as though what the preachers are saying is coming straight from the Almighty.

Little do they know what nature is, but they know what heaven is. If a religion accepts the truth, religious trading will not survive anymore. Nobody will be interested in listening to the preachers once the secret is disclosed.

They pray to him all the time on behalf of us to forgive our sins; but never did God accept their prayers, nor gave a penny to them. Yet, we all, including the governments, always bow down to them. Hence, why will they stop reminding us of the time to catch the flight of paradise?

On a stormy day, the poor are desperate to save their houses, their children, and their belongings. But from their safe haven 'mosques', Imams announce the time of the obligatory prayer. If they truly believed in the Almighty God, then during the storm, they would worship him in open air.

What is the motive of announcing every time, day and night, that Allah is great, and that Muhammad is his messenger? Even a normal person would be irked by such constant and repetitive flattering pronouncements.

Preachers and such are the employees of God. But why do they ask people for money?

And why do they demand religious holidays from humans? They know that God has not allowed them a single day off for he has created them merely to worship him.

You don't have to show your religiousness at a social gathering. A genuine devotee has a quiet place of worship in his or her home. And they know the right time very well.

Honesty is the religion of a true devotee. To live a lifelong honest life — no one has to spend a single moment or a penny or build a house. No cyclone can obstruct anyone's path because one does not have to do anything to be religious; one's conscience should only avoid the path of evil.

True devotees do not follow the path of goodness to go to heaven, they follow it for their self-satisfaction as good human beings. They cannot worship anyone's god. They beg to live in peace, love, and harmony in this wonderful world.

## 2.9 Does the omnipotent Deity depend on humans to implement his divine commandments?

Imams walk around dressed like angels in between one prayer time and the next. They regularly see homeless people sleeping under the sky, in the streets, in the drains and around the luxurious mosques of poor Bangladesh. What do they do for these people? They might say it is not their affair but the government's. Then why are they so anxious to take these people to heaven? What kind of telescope have they invented through which they see Gabriel bringing the message of the Deity?

Seldom do they come to help anybody or participate in any social and scientific activity. They say that scientists are atheists and that Allah will send all atheists to hell. But they gladly use the things made by atheists. First, they prohibit you from using a certain thing by saying that it is not Islamic. But when they find it useful for their religious income, then, after a certain period of time, they cunningly modify the divine commandment and start to use that which was forbidden by them in the first place. But never do they admit that what they and their holy books were saying was wrong. Did they bribe god for this amendment?

Hanging pictures of people, learning languages other than Arabic, and many other things were prohibited for Muslims; but they were later legalised. Can a human being modify divine orders? On the other hand, the clock was invented long ago; however, never have Imams stopped themselves from announcing the time of prayer. Even in this digital age, they continue practising their divine duty more and more noisily.

Their actions demonstrate that god cannot rule the world without them; otherwise, who will lubricate the nuts and bolts of the sun and moon; that is why they say endlessly that god is the most merciful; he will forgive your sins if you pray to him.

Oh, they know the divine verdict of doomsday already!

Indeed, it is an effective theology and a very attractive incentive for religious economic growth; every time you pray to god, your licence to commit more crimes will be automatically renewed.

If he forgives the guilty, what will happen to those who are virtuous?

The priest absolves people of all their sins. Thereby, it is widely seen that those who never or rarely go to the mosque suddenly become mosque-lovers in their old age to eliminate their sins before death by the grace of Imams. These blind worshippers speak every day about the prophet Adam, from whom mankind was born; but they do not learn that even our heavenly father was not pardoned for his sin.

You have to ask yourselves, has god ever forgiven a sinner? Have any theologians changed even a single act of nature by praying in their lifetimes? If the creator had accepted their prayers, the world wouldn't have functioned.

## 2.10 Bribery and temptation may be the principles of preachers but certainly not of divinity.

The creator cannot be something that one can pocket and use to intimidate others. Can you ever blame your religious pundits for misguiding you?

Wherever in Bangladesh bigots see the house of Allah, they probably believe that he is sleeping there, so they do what is told to receive the mercy of the deity.

Sometimes, like a mobile court, a group of preachers come out of a mosque and mainly target the daily wagers and ask them to stop work for a while. Then they speak to them briefly about the lure and punishment of another world, and at last, they say, "There will be nothing left of what you earn here; you must do something for your eternal life; give us whatever you can for Allah's sake, which will last forever and bring you eternal joy after your death."

The poor workers immediately start searching their pockets to bring out all that they have and pay off their debts to the preachers for being born in this world.

The heavenly mobile court proceeds to hunt down others. Not everyone voluntarily gives money for fear of punishment or the temptation of the eternal world — but they do it for the pleasure of the preachers in this world.

They have no intention of leaving this wonderful world. Once they become ill, they forget about their heaven and at once go to atheist physicians.

Little do they know who the creator is, whereas they are the instructors of Godism. Under no circumstances should their bigotry be allowed to be instilled into the minds of innocent people.

## 2.11 Has Allah appointed any of you to act on his behalf?

Taking pictures and watching TV were haram, i.e., forbidden in Islam, but now how are these things permitted? Teaching English and Bengali were also forbidden, but now English has become a halal subject even in madrasahs. Wearing a burka — an outer garment that covers the entire body except for the eyes — is obligatory for Muslim women, but now many of them advocate Islam in public and on TV without wearing burkas. Orthodox Muslim women still put on their traditional burkas, do not watch TV and refuse to be photographed.

That is, they firmly believe that religious or divine doctrines cannot be altered by the evolution of human technology; the faith of Orthodox Muslims is not the same as that of Islamic religious brokers. Getting interest is haram, but Islamic banks and NGOs lend money at a higher interest rate, which does not seem to be haram at all. In our society, only the name of Islam can make everything halal and sanctify every human.

When the Americans land on the moon, Islamist scholars deny it, saying it is anti-Islamic propaganda by non-believers.

But no Islamic dogmatist invented TV for their religious preaching. And from 1969 to date, they have made no magic kite to go to the moon to disprove the existence of the footsteps of non-believers on the moon's surface.

On every occasion, Muslims are used to saying that everything is written in the Quran and that non-Muslims have invented every technology out of it. All blind worshippers also say this quite often. If their claim is true, why have they not invented everything from their holy book?

The Quran is the youngest of all other holy books. It borrowed most of its elements from the Old Commandments (the Bible of Judaism) and the New Commandments (the Bible of Christianity). The Quran recognises all other holy books and the prophets of the Abrahamic religion.

Hajj is one of the fifth obligations of Islam, but no mullah from our land of rivers could invent a steamboat to go to Mecca to fulfil their hajj obligation. Nevertheless, many of them are very specialised in false innovations.

Whenever science advances, religion goes against scientists. When theologians eventually understand in the light of others that their claim was false, they no longer talk about that doctrine. But after a certain period, they invent new dogmas to use the knowledge of non-believers for the sake of believers. That is, they deliberately lie; otherwise, they would have accepted the truth and doubted their holy book as the words of god.

If their religion were true, they would never have killed people for not believing in religion. Everyone knows that god never kills anyone who does not believe in him; yet, we never listen to him but priests.

None of the five pillars of Islam is destined for peace and truthfulness. The first pillar says to believe. The second one says to worship what is said to be believed. The third pillar stands for charity — a rich person must give charity to the poor and this creates a social divide between the rich and the poor. The next one is for fasting, i.e., not eating and drinking during the day, but at night; there is no real difference — only the eating time varies once a year for a lunar month. The fifth pillar says, to perform hajj in Mecca, one has to be rich.

Muslims used to say that the Quran was not burnt in the fire because it was the sacred book of Allah. And devotees too believed it without a doubt. But while other people disbelieved the claim and wanted to see if it really was so, it turned out that the Quran was burning like the other books. Then the Islamists were furious saying that anti-Islam elements were insulting the sanctity of the Quran. And worshippers were protesting against the burning all over the earth.

But none of them raised any questions about their own claim that the sacred book of the Almighty did not catch fire. Do these worshippers believe in Allah or their religious lords? Instead of protesting against the truth, they should have asked themselves whether their claim was true or untrue. If the Quran is proof of God's existence, it could speak for itself; no scholar would be required to clarify any verses of the Quran to humankind.

## 2.12 In this modern age, does the Almighty still come secretly to preachers to give his divine instructions to mankind?

Who gave God and Allah their names? Are these two names of the same creator? If those who disbelieve in God are called infidels by Christians, and if those who disbelieve in Allah are called infidels by Muslims — then are Muslims not infidels in the eyes of Christians, and vice versa? Thus, according to their holy theory, a vast majority of the inhabitants of this earth are, indeed, infidels.

Many self-proclaimed tribal prophets emerged from the same region of the earth to teach humankind the religion of the deities in the Dark Ages. But thereafter, no prophet appeared. In this modern era — it is seen that pastors, bishops, clerics, priests, Imams, and mullahs have become our mini prophets without any proclamation.

That is why in the middle of the night, the Imams on the mike call to us loudly in Bengali, "Wake up, wake up, and go on a fast. Obey the order of Allah." They repeat the words again and again till the time of morning prayers so that people won't be able to sleep but be bound to visit places of worship.

Their motive is that men must go to the mosque. This is the only thing they need to understand — whereas five prayers a day are recited entirely in Arabic, which almost no one, not even many Imams, understand. However, the mosques are mostly overcrowded by worshippers. There are many highly educated professionals among them; how can they, too, perform this ritual blindly without knowing its meaning? In this case, if they could compare themselves with illiterate people, they would understand themselves better.

Who is ordering us to do this — Allah or Imams?

It seems that even in this digital age, the Almighty comes surreptitiously to the Imams and tells them the time for fasting and prayer. And for an emergency order, he sends a text message to a particular Imam; the Imam then broadcasts it to the public from a mosque. Hearing the announcement that someone has insulted their religion, the mobs rush to execute the order of Allah.

Islam says that only Muslims will go to heaven and non-Muslims will go to hell. On the other hand, it says that mankind is the best creation of Allah. If so, don't non-Muslims belong to mankind?

If you talk about an incident on another occasion, Imams question you. But they have been repeating the same old story every day for thousands of years.

People hear every day that nothing happens without Allah's will. If so, why will he be a judge on doomsday? And why do they pray for his forgiveness for their sins?

With your naked eyes, every day and every night, you see that nature has given us everything — the soil, air, water, food …; these are always available free of charge for each being without any distinction; none of this comes from haven to any particular person or community; nor do we get any of this clandestinely through a prophet or preacher. But why do you need someone to tell you what to worship — when and where?

What kind of belief do you cherish in your heart that destroys your conscience? Does god send a messenger to announce the time to evacuate your bowels?

The foundation of religion has taken away our instincts. Only when there is a question of religion do people become so blind that they cannot see with their own eyes; they cannot feel with their own senses; they even hesitate to accept their own truth. They willingly place themselves in the dark, fearing their sins.

Continual dissemination of lies evoking fear and greed by preachers has given them huge power. This really is a very crafty invention of religious leaders, who are actually ruling and distorting the earth behind the government's back without even being elected by the people.

## 2.13 If one wants to know the truth, does it hurt religious sentiments?

Studying science is obviously hurting religious sentiments, isn't it? Christianity says, "God speaks through the Bible"; Islam says, "God speaks through the Quran", which the former does not accept. So, which one speaks the truth?

Theologians do not have knowledge of an ant, but every day they tell us thrilling stories of its creator. They enjoy everything on this magnificent earth but always talk about heaven that they have not experienced for themselves. Their preaching will never end until they can transform every place on earth into the house of god. Only then will they be able to transfer us to heaven as there will be no more place left here to sleep and eat.

Looking at all these inconceivably wonderful creations of nature, if you still cannot appreciate them but believe in someone's words, then what value does your faith have for you?

Out of your fear, you accept that someone is looking after you to tell you what to do. You have your life to live, not anyone else's. Once you realise that you are solely responsible for yourself, you will have the vitality and vigour to make your own path. For that, you must have a mind and heart that is completely free from all the burdens of life.

If this world did not exist, no one would think about it. The thoughts of the believers and unbelievers lean towards the creation of this mysterious universe. These people at least meditate upon its wonders. This expresses their adoration.

The second type of people are those who do not use their instincts; instead, they believe what is told by their religious masters. These people are blind followers, and they mostly support dishonest élite people under the umbrella of religion, which is the utmost safe haven for them.

The worst people are those who think that they nourish god and are the guardians of godism. They are very fearful of reasoning and contemplation. Therefore, cowards always want to kill those who question them to know the truth.

An owner of pure gold would never hesitate or run away if she was asked any questions about the authenticity of her gold. If she is asked, she naturally answers all the relevant questions; the more you doubt, the more she is delighted, her eyes gleaming and face smiling; she does not run away. Even if you grab the gold from her possession and rub it for as long as you can, every particle of it will tell you the same truth.

But the owner of fake gold will disappear from the scene, or if he has a mob behind him, he will talk irrelevantly about something else.

Those who lie but do not force others to believe what they say are not as bad as those who lie premeditatedly and have the power to make others believe that their words are true; these people are extremely dangerous to all humankind.

## 2.14 There is no communal violence in nature; there is diversity and individual freedom everywhere.

Since there are many self-contradictory doctrines in religion, it is indeed very difficult to get on the right path of knowledge. Doubts are naturally born out of doubtful doctrines.

If people truly believe in the creator, then it is not difficult to choose the right path without going through the holy book. I mean the path of goodness against badness, on which perhaps the conscience of all humans is based.

If you simply question yourself why so many contradictory religious doctrines exist even in the same religion, you can lucidly find the answer. For these doctrines came from human beings, not from any deity.

Here is an actual dilemma for me to understand the relationship between different deities and religions as I know that there is no religion without a god or whatever.

*There are people who unconsciously interpret Buddhism as a religion; in fact, it is not; it is merely the teachings of Siddhartha Gautama Buddha, his experience in real life without the involvement of any god. Millennia ago, Buddha emphatically respected the lives of all animals equally. His practice of wisdom and compassion gave an unparalleled message to humankind.*

I believe that a conscientious person can easily understand that religions were created by people for their good. But what comes afterwards from the preachers is all dogmas, which confuse the common people about god and religion.

Why does a religious scholar disagree with his fellow scholar if they are the real scholars of heaven? Even about the same thing in the same religion, they talk very differently as though they are adversaries of one another. But they become great friends when it comes to protecting their monopoly of trade on earth as protectors of heaven.

Nature is a unique knowledge laboratory for all beings. It is full of wonders. It is beyond the comprehension of any human being. We do not know its beginning or its end. The more you look into it, the more you disappear into its depths.

If the creator, as defined by the preachers, really exists and wants to say something about his religion to the inhabitants of the earth, he has every capacity to appear before his people anywhere and speak to them in any language. I doubt a human being can play such a role on behalf of the creator.

The sun does not rise for any specific person; it rises evenly for each and every being.

We, humans, are very undisciplined and biased. Many other animals have good senses, which we do not try to realise because of our self-importance. You can learn plentiful things from nature without being a scholar.

Other animals have the same god as we humans have. But what religion(s) do they follow? Even in this ultra-modern civilised world, every human being is born naked and poor. No matter which rich family you belong to, you could not bring a simple piece of cloth with you at birth. And when we die, our rich, scented corpses are eaten by poor insects. This is the reality of human life.

The origin of all animals including humans is always the same: coming fully naked into this world and leaving it likewise.

Can you find anyone rich or poor in another animal's society? There is no slavery in the kingdom of beasts. But our god himself authorised the system of slavery in the religions of humans.

After a very long period of the Stone Age, humans were able to successfully create 'division of labour' that heralded the start of the classification of the rich and the poor, and so our civilisation began to take shape. Since then, religious leaders have not gone hunting for food. For they were cleverly able to give that responsibility to naïve peasants; so that priests could spawn dogma after dogma from the so-called house of god, and the peasants could bring food right up to the priests' table to receive their benedictions to reach heaven.

A lot of people in this world do not have their own place to sleep. On an occasion or two, the clerics distribute charity among the poor from the house of god; thereafter, they lock the door. To expose such kindness to god, they always need the poor in society; the rich will not survive with the word 'rich' otherwise.

On the other hand, the animal kingdom is always as it is. Interestingly, they did not have a charitable system in the primitive era, nor do they have such a system in this modern age. They still eat in an uncivilised manner, and they still leave their food for others as soon as their stomachs are full. They never store food in a warehouse to profit from it later. They too own this god-gifted land, don't they?

Animals are completely free; true liberty exists in their societies. They do not gang up to interfere in other animals' affairs. Many beasts have amazing knowledge. A hen, typically poor and stupid, always runs here and there to hunt for food; once they have been spawned, they are something different.

When a hen begins to hatch her eggs, she continuously sits on them for several days without having food and all the rest. While she births her chicks, she rears them so gently and never leaves them alone. If she sees someone or another animal nearby, the dumb hen immediately starts to make loud noises (their language probably). At once, more than a dozen of her little kids run and hide in their mother's feathers. If she feels any immediate danger to her children, she does not hesitate to attack the enemies. She continues alerting them until the danger is over. Sometimes sweet chicks peep through the protection of feathers. The mother is constantly alert and careful. One day when she notices that her little ones have grown up, she lets them go freely into nature to find their own path.

If we do not have the knowledge of a simple little egg, it does not matter. Since we know a lot, our biggest problem, however, is that we do not know what we do not know. The unsophisticated brains of beasts perhaps know that their knowledge is limited; we think ours is infinite.

But just look at an egg, not at the universe. Does any theologian or scientist know if an egg or a chicken came first? From what element of nothingness, were they created?

## 2.15 Each human can independently understand the language of nature without interpretation by dint of any human language.

If you close your eyes for a while, you will see clearly and feel that nature speaks in its own language.

Whether nature acts on its own or any supernatural person rules it — we do not know. Nonetheless, some people can feel and believe its effectiveness in many logical and reasonably imaginable ways. That is why there are different beliefs about the ultimate truth. But as long as superstition is believed in the human brain, never will they be able to lay an egg.

Did people put faith in god after seeing the so-called sacred books?

Did the omniscient god need any human language and human help to reveal his holy book?

If the creator wanted to say something in writing to mankind, do you not think he could have done it long before paper was invented by humans?

On the day of our divine judgement, if one dares to say that dear God, I was not able to choose what they called the right path because I could neither speak nor could I read. And many others did not even know that these religious doctrines existed.

What will our distinguished divine scholars say then?

Beware of false prophets! They are inwardly ravening wolves but come to you in sheep's clothing.

How can religion have anything to do with the truth when it is founded on a fallacy? The parochialism of human society helps people live in confinement in the dark.

To believe in the supernatural, one must have a profound knowledge of nature. Albert Einstein understood the language of nature and said, "Look deep into nature, and then you will understand everything better."

Many governments on this earth take oaths in the name of their respective religious deities. Does it mean that god recognises them as his shadow ministers? I guess the creator has not created any countries but the world.

The communal acts of worshipping god may make people religious, but the personal act of goodness makes people virtuous.

For the greed of reaching the land of heaven, why should we live hellish lives on our magnificent earth?

The wonders of the world for many are buildings or statues — the tallest, oldest or most beautiful.

Everywhere in the world, nature is full of unbelievable and inconceivable wonders! We cannot see them all; we cannot know them all. But we want to learn about them. Perhaps — one day — we will see some of them through our experiences on the long journey towards death.

Every little being is so impressive, so inspiring, and so marvellous; it is simply impossible to express the bounties and beauty of nature.

For those who have seen the outstanding beauty of a dark night sitting under a tranquil deep blue sky or have listened to the serenity of a charismatic forest, or who have once had the experience of watching its captivating eye-catching performance sitting alone on the banks of a natural river — at that moment one may find oneself in a virtual standstill — which scenery is the most wonderful, or which is the oldest — it is impossible to compare.

## 2.16 How did Christianity know the first man on earth, whereas they did not even know about the existence of the continent of America and its people until the end of the 15th century?

Even before 1492, civilised European Christians did not have knowledge of the existence of a continent on this earth, but how did they know that its first man descended from heaven?

As Christianity was born out of a religion that existed previously in Jerusalem, Palestine, did god make any mistakes in Judaism that led to the creation of Christianity? And Judaism originated from Abraham, whose parents were pagans who worshipped multiple gods. One day their son came to believe in the one god doctrine. Jesus himself was a Jew and was later known as the founder of Christianity. And eventually, Islam was founded on the same roots that made it one of the three main Abrahamic religions.

Historically, it appears that the Old Testament of the Prophet Moses (the Torah, the Hebrew Bible) became the New Testament of Christians; thanks to Saint Paul, a Jewish-turned-Christian, Jesus' first follower and preacher of Christianity — for establishing a Western religion from a sect of polytheistic tribal faiths in the desert.

Abrahamic religious history in the holy books is all about the Jerusalem-centric people of that time even though — at that time and before that — much transpired elsewhere in the world — where the ubiquitous deity said nothing — and he says nothing about what happened after that era. Is god really omnipresent or omniabsent?

The West of Christianity does not recognise any religion other than theirs. Many of their countries do not accept Hinduism as a religion; may be because in Hinduism, women have roles of goddesses that do not exist in the Abrahamic religions.

The religion of ancient Hindustan (India) is Hindu, and a native of India is also known as a Hindu; thus, the word Hindu signifies the inhabitants of the country as well as the adherents of Hinduism. Hinduism, however, does not believe in preaching, unlike Christianity and Islam. Many prehistoric religions have disappeared from this world. The oldest religion that exists in this world is Hinduism. The evidence of its earliest scriptures, hence, contradicts Bible's view of creation of the world.

Before any religion was founded, people had been living for hundreds and thousands of years; and those who cannot read and write their own language even in this modern age, will they not go to hell?

But who will be accountable for this — God or the prophets? On the day of our celestial judgement, those seers might say that they were not responsible for this.

The worshippers may then say, "Oh, our most merciful, gracious, loving Lord, we did what these preachers asked us to do on earth, as they were acting on behalf of you; throw them into hell at once."

If god replies, "Oh, my dear believers, do not worry; hell is waiting for you."

## 2.17 The existence of a single lie or mistake is enough to distrust any holy book because the creator that people believe in cannot lie nor do anything wrong.

Men have always fought among themselves for their superiority complex, but they turn into a single force against other creatures. This is a typical example of human arrogance, which is seen repeatedly in society.

Mankind has many religions within the single god doctrine; many of their statements are self-contradictory. One of their lies becomes the evidence of their previous lies. To cover up a lie, multiple lies are born as witnesses to a single lie.

Christianity was born based on a rumour. Miriam (Mary), a natural person, gave a virgin birth to the Son of God. Why did God need a human to give birth to his holy son? He could have easily dropped Jesus from heaven, as he did in the case of Adam and Eve. Still, it was a pity that Mary was not worshipped as the Goddess of Christians. A virgin Hebrew girl did such a great divine job for Christianity, but no woman is allowed to head their church.

In history, Jesus was a Jew and was killed by trained Roman soldiers in their system of crucifixion. His followers were first dismayed at this because a messiah, as the Jews believed, just could not be murdered in such a humiliating fashion. At this emotional juncture of their belief, clever Paul, a Jew, had a miraculous idea that convinced many frustrated Bedouins in the desert under Roman occupation to believe that Jesus had risen from the dead. Their organisation, known as the Church, was born from this belief. Thence, they tactically succeeded in convincing Emperor Constantine to convert to Christianity. Thus, the power of the Roman Empire was taken over by the Church; as a result, a new religious faith that originated from old Judaism rapidly spread and became popular throughout the Roman Empire.

During religious wars and wars for women within tribal communities, preaching for a new religion significantly increased the demand for Christianity in that part of the world in Jerusalem — then under the occupation of the Roman Empire. Paul preached Christianity in the name of Jesus as God and the Son of God himself. If he had preached Christianity in his name instead of Jesus, people would not have believed him. This clever policy of Saint Paul led many people to believe in Christianity, which allowed the tribal religion of a community to become the religion of the West.

The beliefs of the Church, by that time, had moved decisively away from the old faith of Jews, which their founders had never contemplated. In order to clarify their new faith as Christians, the Fathers of the Church established a new scripture, the so-called New Testament (Christian Bible), which they claimed superseded the written Torah and called it the 'Old' Testament. But to Jews, it is only the 'Bible' (the term Hebrew Bible is used to distinguish it from the new Bible of Christians). It is said in Judaism that the Jewish prophet Moses received the Ten Commandments from God on the top of Mount Sinai in Egypt.

And much later, Islam emerged as a new and last Abrahamic religion. Prophet Muhammad, an Arab, claimed to have become a new and final prophet. A new sacred book, the Quran — a collection of revelations for Muslims as a new belief — was eventually introduced that partially believes in the Torah, the Bible, and all the other holy books and prophets of Abrahamic religions.

What we ordinary people understand from all these holy texts is that one of them is a rival of the other. But what does God say to humankind about his sacred texts? Is he the same God for these three Abrahamic religions?

The faith in a single god originated from Abraham whose parents were polytheists. A similar message was subsequently carried forward by Moses, Jesus and Muhammad. The Quran borrowed elements from the holy books of Judaism and Christianity as well as made past references to Adam and Eve.

What religion did Muhammad believe in before founding Islam? If he was a Jew or a Christian, was he not an infidel in the eyes of his new religion? If he did not believe in any religion before Islam, was he not an atheist?

Judaism spawned out of polytheistic tribal faiths in the desert. The Jewish scriptures are filled with seers who were ill-treated. It is said that god sent many prophets one by one because people were bad then. This tells us that the prophets of the Dark Ages made all people righteous and that no more bad people existed on this earth; consequently, these seers have all gone back to heaven. But what are the fathers, bishops, pastors, priests, clerics and Imams doing here in these modern times? Are they replacements of those prophets?

One of the Wonders of the Old World was one of the Greek gods — Helios — a statue of the Colossus at Rhodes. Ancient Greek gods and goddesses ruled every aspect of human life from the highest mountain in Greece.

In polytheistic societies, people worshipped man as god, and there were many gods. At that time, people practised infanticide, i.e., human sacrifice to a godhead. Islam, too, was born in a polytheistic society. Muhammad, who founded the religion in early seventh century, eventually removed all other gods and goddesses from the Ka'ba. Subsequently, many other sects stemmed from Islam — Shia, Sunni, Ibadi, Wahhabi and so on — just as Christianity was divided into Catholic, Protestant, Latter-day Saints and so forth.

The Ka'ba was originally the sacred house of the Bedouin tribes; they worshipped many idols of pagan deities there. After the conquest of Mecca by Muhammad, all the idols including the picture of Miriam with the little Messiah of Israel were removed from there, and it became the holy site of his followers in the region; then they identified themselves as Mohammedans (Muslims). Soon after, Islam spread throughout the Arabian Peninsula.

The Ka'ba — the birthplace of many idols of gods and goddesses — became the worship place of a non-idolatrous god for Muslims; then the almighty made it mandatory for wealthy mankind to visit it once a lunar year.

After abolishing the place of worship of the Bedouin tribal religion, how could the same Ka'ba become the sacred house of the Islamic god?

As god is defined as ubiquitous, why do Muslims face in the direction of the Ka'ba to pray? Is the prophet more respectful than Allah?

Abraham (Ibrahim), a Hebrew and founder of Judaism, was about to kill his son for the will of God, who appeared to him in a dream. Abraham's story becomes the centre of the new religion, although the story is told differently in Islamism.

Practising infanticide was, indeed, very agonising. Later, people started sacrificing sheep as a religious duty, resulting in a mutton feast being held for Muslims. Only sheep and camels were mainly found in the deserts of that part of the world.

The scarceness of lambs, the invention of ropes, and sharp instruments for tying and killing big animals led people to gradually shift attention to other beasts for slaughtering for god's will. But have humans created beasts so that they can sacrifice them to fulfil god's will?

Look at its irony. How can the 'sacrifice' of innocent victims, i.e., torture and murder, be a good thing? Can compassion have anything to do with this belief?

## 2.18 Is it so easy to understand the creator(s) of this universe?

How can a little child become a follower of a religion while he or she still does not understand his or her parents well? Even many parents do not know the fundamentals and history of the religion they follow. Most people are followers of a religion because they were born into that one. Before worshipping the holy book, people are not first asked to read and comprehend what it says.

Children are naturally very curious as their brain is very fresh, pure and empty without prejudice. Once they start talking, they ask one question after another. The parents reply with joy when they notice that their kids are geniuses. The children then question further with interest, but the answer they get is:

Don't say this again!

Why papa?

Don't ask such questions. God will punish you.

You've said that god created us, but why can't I ask who created god?

Because it's a great sin.

Papa, wasn't it a sin when I asked you who created us?

You're becoming so stupid! God will definitely throw you into hell.

What's hell, mum?

It's where you will be burning for all your eternal life.

The child looks at his mother with startled eyes, cries, and falls asleep on her lap.

The fear of religion makes pure innocent children dumb in our society. In this way, their sharp intellect is nipped in the bud.

Never do I understand a simple creature. I am a human being; I ask myself how so many children can understand god so easily.

The holy book talks about the theory of creation like a fairy tale. There are many fragmented statements and irrational arguments. Islamic scholars justify this because the Quran is the book of God, so it does not follow the pattern of traditional human books. If their reasoning is correct, will the non-traditional books of humans who do not write the traditional way be considered the books of God?

Did religious scholars receive their degrees from the school of heaven to know the mind of the Deity?

The creator may talk to whomever he pleases, but can he secretly reveal his sacred book to a man for all human beings? Since the deity does not speak to humankind except preachers, people do not argue with him but with preachers. Are blatant liars and sinners better than non-believers?

The book of heaven says that Adam was unfaithful to god; as a penalty, he was sent to earth. But how did a sinful man become the prophet of mankind?

The Quran says that it is the word of Allah, yet it itself proves that it is the word of a man who says that he has received the messages from God for mankind. The verses of the Quran were long remembered by his followers, long after his death before it appeared as a holy book. Prophet Muhammad could not read and write his mother tongue (Arabic). So, he needed others whom he instructed to recall and write divine messages in stone and elsewhere. However, who verified that it was the word of God?

The prophet who claimed that he had travelled to the Seven Heavens by the miraculous power of Allah but could not write the deity's messages in his mother tongue! Was it not a great pity that the omniscient creator was not capable of writing his holy book, so he asked a man for help to reveal it?

It is said that the objective of the Quran is to make man aware of the Creation plan of God. But do they believe that the Almighty was gossiping with one of his creations about the creation plan of this universe? I believe that a man can talk to other people about a transistor, but will the man ever gossip with the transistor about how and why he made it?

The sacred books of God (and Allah) say that he created the whole universe in six days. Since there was no 'day' before creation, where did those six days come from?

It is also stated in the Bible and the Quran that the earth does not move, it stands firm — God holds it.

Scientists, however, say that the earth orbits around the sun. How could such contradictory theories of the same thing exist in the educational institutions of the world, where humans are the best and most intelligent creatures?

I wonder how — the most gracious God — can say that he has created mankind to worship him. It sounds like a purely human character. Still, I do not reckon even a sensible carpenter would ever tell a chair to worship him.

When one sees a tree blossom, an impulsive admiration automatically comes out of one's heart; the flower does not oblige anyone to do anything for its wonderful being.

No one in the world doubts a leaf of the tree; when people see such a leaf, everyone's mind at once, I suppose, says that divinity is there. But why do their minds not react in the same way when they see a leaf from the holy book?

## 2.19 Why is there warfare between knowledge and religion?

A theory of science can be argued openly and with interest, but why not theology? It is often heard in a religious discourse (owas mahafil) that Ibrahim (Abraham) dreamed a dream that god was telling him to sacrifice his best-loved one. For fulfilling the will of God, Ibrahim was in the moment of killing his son; while he was wielding a knife to his son's throat, he suddenly noticed that there was a sheep there instead of his son.

If it was so, people should have continued to sacrifice their sons; each time, a beloved son could have been saved, and instead, a sheep appeared as a gift from god. In addition, a great sacrifice for a religious duty could be fulfilled.

Why didn't Abraham sacrifice himself to god's will?

In 1600, the Italian natural philosopher Giordano Bruno was burnt alive in Rome by the Fathers of the Church because he said that the Earth was moving, which is against biblical theology, that is, against God. Therefore, in the eyes of the inquisitors, it was a huge sin. Knowing or telling the truth can be a sin for heresy, but can it be for divinity?

So, why do Christians believe in this? Did the inquisitors execute God's commands, or were they Gods themselves?

Interestingly, Bruno's contrasting view of the world stemmed from his own religious beliefs in Christianity. Nevertheless, he was convicted as an infidel. He was burnt at the stake in public by the Catholic Church to please their god. They watched ecstatically how an infidel was burning alive. This act undoubtedly reveals that their god punishes whoever speaks to know the truth, but he forgives all the deceivers if they worship him through the Bible.

It is said that Adam (the first man) and Eve (the second of mankind) were living eternally in heaven. They were allowed to enjoy everything there except eating fruits from a certain apple tree, which was reserved for God. But the eyes of Eve (Hawa) were staring at the forbidden tree; one day, she eventually ate an apple and asked Adam to share it, and then he did too. They both disobeyed God. As a punishment, they were dismissed from heaven.

This is why all other humans, god's best creatures, lost heaven where many beautiful fairies were supposedly waiting to serve them as slaves. That is why they always pray to go back there.

But who made Adam the prophet of mankind for the crime he committed against God?

As we know from religious history that a bunch of seers were sent to earth to teach the religion of god as the people were bad then, so being the first human, was Adam a prophet of his own?

In prehistoric times, humans, like other animals, had been living in caves for thousands and thousands of years. Throughout the beginning of the age of primitive mankind, humans had been eating like beasts; they had not even thought about how to light a fire. And in the Stone Age, without theologians and scientists, these indigenous people were able to discover fire by rubbing stone after stone.

It was those pure, natural, illiterate, and profane people who paved the path of cooking and eating. The blacksmiths began to make hand instruments for hunting, and the potters introduced pots for cooking. Since then, human civilisation had begun. To understand this, no knowledge from books was required. And today to visualise the very primitive times of humans, you need nothing; just look back at them with your mind; you will see everything lucidly. There was no history there; no human being could read and write for long periods during the Stone Age.

And much before the Stone Age, what was Prophet Adam doing and eating? In which cave was he living as the first man on this earth? No human language existed at that time; reading or writing was unimaginable. If he really were the first human in the world, then those first aboriginals were his children. But how was it possible that they did not know about god and his religion?

## 2.20 Animals, except humans, never work against nature.

Nature is totally free, for each and every being. True liberty exists in the natural environment. Every natural geographical region on this earth is alike, different, unique and incredibly beautiful. You can copy many things from nature, which is the purpose of its being; but you cannot do anything as a true copy from it.

All humans are animals, but not all animals are humans. A tiger can be a danger to humans, and the dharma of the tiger is known. On the other hand, a human can be abundantly dangerous to another human; you can never be sure of the nature of your fellow humans.

The human mind is naturally always on the side of the truth, but their head is on the side of falsehood perhaps because of society. Human society is an artificial one. What they say about themselves at home is different from what they say outside; the way they dress at home and the way they dress at a festival are not the same.

Except for human society, all other animal societies are pure and authentic. They do not face any such problems that we face. Never do they go against nature, but we do.

The sense of right and wrong arises from the constitution of our mind, not from a book. Books are there for knowing others. When there was no book, people were still intelligent and humane. A dog is very intelligent and kind, but I do not think dogs go to school or read any human language.

Even in this modern world, tons of people still cannot read and write their own language; one community does not know the language of another. Once upon a time, no one could read because people did not know how to write. Once those illiterate people were able to invent writing methods, then, others could be educated. Do you need any evidence to believe this?

Many beasts, physically and intelligently, always serve humans for free; moreover, they sacrifice themselves for the pleasure of man. But no tiger or any other animal has ever sacrificed a human being for the pleasure of God.

When beasts are taken to murder, they understand the intention of the men. It is unbearable to look into the affectionate eyes of those innocent dumb beasts in the scene; they too have lives like ours; they are also the creatures of god; they cry and try to escape from the spot. But the men tie them so cruelly, slit their throat so joyfully, and strip off their skin to make our shoes. Then we celebrate the feast. This is our sacrifice for our loving God. But will he ever believe us?

You can sacrifice yourself if you want. But does your conscience permit you to slaughter other innocent lives in the name of god? You can purify your heart if it is not holy; but can you sanctify anything which is not yours?

When we talk about ourselves, we pompously say my race is superior to yours; our country is the best, and theirs is the worst.

I + I = we = they = you =? The same 'I' always changes itself from one situation to another in conflicting ways. Can you imagine how the human brain plays with words, and what effect this has on society?

The south cannot be compared with the north or the east with the west since they always lie opposite of each other and are geographically different from one another.

Beasts never lie. Dogs adore their human masters and never betray them; yet you hate a dog simply because it is a dog — but you love a zealot because he or she is a human.

Humans are creatures like other animals. While birds talk to each other, we do not understand their language, so we think that they cannot communicate.

When the mating season begins, many weaverbirds build their nests by weaving fine strong leaves, fibres, grass, and twigs together.

They thoughtfully choose a straight tall tree like a coconut one. They are indefatigable workers. The way they work, it seems they are playing and singing together. Their pendulous home engineering commences with a single strand, which is knotted chiefly to a branch of the Palmyra tree (in Asia). A downwards long tube, a narrow entrance and a chamber that functions as a nursery, are made. They do all this just using their beaks.

Their material collection process, ideal design, and complex weaving techniques are incredibly impressive. Even a weaver would be surprised if he or she attentively watches this intellectual capability and creativity of these birds. There is no such thing as arrogance; none receives a medal.

How an ant sends a signal to their community without making any noise and disturbing others is still unthinkable for mankind.

Bees work together brilliantly to create their hanging home. No man, however intelligent they may be, can make such a nest. The hanging bee nest is naturally soft and has many layers and compartments; it is incredible architecture. It is amazing to see how these tiny sophisticated engineers work, with no pollution. This is natural engineering! The way they collect readymade materials from nature and how they perform their respective work is unbelievable. People sometimes say, "I was as busy as a bee." I wonder if they remember what type of brain a tiny bee has and what technology they use. The instinct of bees is inconceivable and incomprehensible to human beings.

Birds are brilliantly self-disciplined. Migratory birds travel thousands of kilometres from one continent to another each year without any travel documents. They meet together in a quiet place; at the end of their seasonal voyage, they intelligently fly in huge flocks to return to their destinations.

I wonder again and again how the birds communicate among themselves and organise such long flights so quietly without disturbing others and polluting the world. How do they navigate, observe and choose charming natural surroundings that will not be dangerous to them, and what resolution do they take before they leave?

They are almost certain of places where they will not be attacked by other animals — but not always sure about humans. Civilised people may not eat these birds; their hobby, nonetheless, is to kill innocents for pleasure.

A cow naturally gives birth by herself and instantly starts licking the young; only a few minutes after it is born, the calf is on its feet and ready to run. Ever since the beginning of human society, people have been feeding on cow's milk; farmers have been using cows for ploughing the land, transporting things as well as transporting people and for many other purposes. Even cow dung has always been used as fuel for cooking and as a natural fertiliser for farming; it is also used to protect and varnish the mud floor. Furthermore, a cow sacrifices its flesh, skin, legs, bones, and every part of it for the pleasure of man.

The greatness of a cow is unique. No great human is comparable to the skin of a cow. Perhaps this is why many treat them with great devotion; however, many feel that it is silly to have such respect for cows. It is, indeed, a difference in the mentality and spirituality of the people belonging to different geographical regions of this world.

Is it not ridiculous to call some pieces of written paper a sacred book, and then worship it?

## 2.21 Can a human define the creator? Deceiving people in the name of God is the greatest sin of mankind.

I cannot imagine how theologians who still do not know the beginning and end of the universe define its creator and convincingly explain his creation plan to us. Fairy tales are much better than religious credos. These divine intellects have locked themselves up in the diminutive houses of deity — from where they can possibly see the Seven Heavens, but unfortunately, do not see the beauty of nature.

Those who say that there is no creator, and those who say that there is only one; the question, however, is how do they know? If there were no creator, nothing would exist; since the world exists, something must have been mysteriously created by itself, which is beyond human reasoning.

It could be anything. Or who knows; maybe it always was.

What is nothingness, and how much is it worth? And where is it?

Suspicion stems from one's suspicious behaviour. Dishonest people do not come from another planet. Why was God unable to appear before his human race — but secretly come to speak to only one man at a time?

Did the word 'God' ever exist in Abrahamic religion? Elohim, Allah, and all the rest — these names were known by various seers for their distinctive religions.

See the irony of it. Each religion is different and has its own idea of the creator(s). The term 'God' may have been trickily coined by the latter-day scholars of believers, in order to bring all herds to worship a common name regardless of the existence of diverse deities in their respective sacred texts. Thus, the word God is actually seen as the name of a religious cartel of different faiths.

If the same creator had indeed spoken to those prophets to explain his longing for mankind, it would have been impossible to have so many religions within the doctrine of a single God. History has shown that God is the enemy of Allah, and vice versa. When a war breaks out between two countries or groups, one of them says, "Allah is on our side," and the other says, "God is with us"; while one wins the war, what happens to the Almighty on the defeated side?

## 2.22 Goodness is the work of divinity, and it is the name of true religion.

The teaching of our ancestors was that the individual goodness of a person leads to the goodness of the entire society.

If god has really created a religion by name, it could be attributed to the goodness of each human being. If you think that you will be able to reach heaven as a follower of Islam, then why will the day of divine judgement arrive? And that judgement cannot be based on one's religion, but on one's actions, i.e., karma.

If 'peace' is a fundamental principle of our religion, then pacifists of any religion and non-religion also follow at least one of our religious principles; but do we show respect for them? Not really, our love for a bad person of our religion is much more than that of a good person of another religion. Do you reckon this could be the dharma of divinity?

Personal relations between different faiths are always nice and amicable everywhere in the world. But once a communal issue arises, this splendid relationship turns into acrimony, not because of the individual but because of their organisation. Ordinary people do not support violence, but not many oppose it tangibly. Some individuals, however, come forward bravely and go against their communal mobs to defend vulnerable communities. But these righteous persons immediately become enemies of their own communities and are accused: "Being one of our own, how can you protect people of other religions?" Institutional hatred and injustice in the name of religion is a serious and persistent threat to the morality of human society.

How can those who hate others simply because of difference in faiths believe that humans are god's best creation? Religio-politicians are extremely poisonous elements. They often purposefully inflame communal violence, on the other hand, cunningly telling the public that violent people have no religion, whereas those people are the protectors of their own religion.

In every aspect of our life, we always ask a lot of questions; in contrast, when our religious pundits talk to us, we come to a total standstill!

For all of us, it is our moral duty to be fully aware of the religious actors in society so that they can no longer use religion as their property and political weapon. Only then will the religion-loving ordinary people be freed from religious blindness and religious madness.

We, perhaps, do not contemplate our religiousness. If the intention of a good deed is bad, then it is obviously an evil act. One can worship the creator to show sincere gratitude for this marvellous world but expect nothing in return. A true devotee always lives a life of truth for a peaceful mind and happiness; this person is certainly not afraid of any imaginary things; he can ask questions, search, and follow his own path to reach the ultimate truth in his lifetime.

In his long open-door journey, he may encounter many people with many minds in different and alike environments; he may get lost; he may go wrong; he may cast doubt on his original path and yet may hold back. He may come across many mysterious thoughts, but the real experience he earns along the way is his own; he may not find the truth of all the truth, but he will certainly become confident. This is what the creator may expect from a human. If you believe he is the creator of this universe, what else can you offer him?

Turning knowledge into wisdom can lead you towards the true path of self-confidence. Ignorance and superstition can only make you dependent on deceivers and bigots.

## 2.23 If you need a human to know the creator, what is the charisma of the almighty?

The followers of one religion say everything is found through faith — not through arguments; if so, why don't they believe in other people's faiths? With what logic do they claim that their religion is true and establish their reasoning against other religions?

Instead of going to war against other believers, why don't they exchange their true findings with them to accept the only truth?

It is not a question of believing or not believing the holy book, but of whether it is the book of god.

Scientists know about the heart, but the mind means nothing to them; other people have been practising deeply since ancient times to focus their minds.

Genuine religious gurus should normally be more knowledgeable than scientists; — as it is assumed that where the knowledge of science stops, there begins the knowledge of spirituality.

You need to know the language of a writer to read a book; conversely, you need no language to read nature. If you read a book, you know what its author says. If you read nature, you know what nature says. If you want to talk to someone, you need to know the language of the person. But you can speak to nature without knowing any language. This is the charisma of the creator.

Chapter 3

# Some Words from the Past

## 3.1 Can those who refuse to say Jai Bangla claim that they were Mukti Bahini (freedom fighters)?

In 1971, ordinary Bengalis in Pakistan hoped that things would get better after their victory as an independent nation; unfortunately, vital things began to worsen.

The true spirit of the guerrilla war for which the nation earned its own historical identity was washed away right after independence, which deeply undermined the authentic principles and visions of the freedom fighters known as Mukti Bahini.

I remember that fateful night spent in Dacca on March 25, 1971 (now it is spelt Dhaka in the Latin alphabet, the Bengali spelling remains as it is in Bengali letters). On that day, Bengali freedom fighters were born predominantly among the ordinary people of all communities when we initiated a guerrilla war by roaring *Jai Bangla* to liberate our Bengali nation.

The Pakistan Awami Muslim League (PAL), a Bengali nationalist party led by Sheikh Mujibur Rahman, won a landslide victory in the national elections (December 1970), which gave PAL the constitutional right to form an absolute government for the whole of Pakistan. But Pakistan People's Party (PPP) leader Zulfiqar Ali Bhutto, a left-wing and democratic socialist party that emerged as the second largest majority in the elections, was unwilling to give Mujib absolute power over Pakistan.

Since the PAL failed to win any seat in West Pakistan, on the other hand, the PPP failed to win any seat in East Pakistan, thus Bhutto proposed to form a coalition government between them, but Mujib refused.

Since the creation of Pakistan in 1947, it has had five provinces, viz., 1. Punjab, 2. Sindhu, 3. Baluchistan, 4. North-West Frontier Province = West Pakistan and 5. East Bengal. Eight years after, in 1955, the provincial name of East Bengal in Pakistan was erased and renamed East Pakistan.

The principles of representation were made based on populations; since the population of East Pakistan was more than the combined population of the four provinces of West Pakistan, the former got more than half the seats in the National Assembly of Pakistan. Therefore, although PAL could not win any seats from West Pakistan, it won a majority of seats in the National Assembly of entire Pakistan. Nevertheless, Bhutto declined to allow Mujib to become the Prime Minister of Pakistan with the influence and power of General Yahya Khan's military government.

This election remarkably states from the point of view of the common people in both wings of Pakistan that religion was only a pretext used by evil-minded religio-politicians to create Pakistan. And this was the turning point in starting a civil war within the Muslim fraternity; this empirically proves that there was a nefarious design behind its creation from India. Now Muslims are fighting against each other — we are Bengalis, and they are Biharis, Punjabis, Baluchis, and Sindhis, but we and they are both Muslims — this issue is thrown away at this point in time.

In the aftermath of this momentum, on March 7, 1971, Mujib addressed a huge crowd that had filled the entire Ramna Racecourse Maydan and beyond that. The crowd had turned themselves into a massive irresistible force, led by the then furious student movement.

After that day, the civil administrations in the Eastern province were virtually paralysed. The brave speech of Bangabandhu Sheikh Mujibur Rahman eloquently articulated two options for the military government: either you immediately hand over power to the winner of the elections, or we will free our country from you by any means possible.

This was the declaration of independence. To resolve this grave situation, Bhutto and President Yahya came to Dhaka (Dacca) and held several meetings with Mujib for a political solution, but power-sharing talks between the two sides failed. This led to that horrific nightmare of March 25, 1971; Mujib was arrested and taken to West

Pakistan; the army started a military intervention against the unforgettable spirit of the Bengali nation.

The unexpected nightmare of that day actually drove the Bengalis to go against the West Pakistanis and begin a guerrilla war by forming Mukti Bahini. Before that day, East Pakistan never wanted to separate from West Pakistan, except to demand political autonomy for the province.

Though the speech of pre-Bangladesh Mujib was the main inspiration to begin the civil war, it does not mean that all the freedom fighters and those who passionately supported our independence were the people of PAL. But at that time, no one except Mujib was in a position to declare formal independence for Bangladesh. At that juncture, most people from all walks of life clearly realised that the rights of the Bengalis had been unjustly denied. Patriotic people who were mainly students, unemployed youths, various professionals and non-professionals who quit their jobs joined the guerrilla warfare without any distinction, whether it was religion or political parties. In the meantime, Lieutenant-General Tikka Khan was appointed governor of East Pakistan.

Only in less than nine months, we snatched our freedom from the domination of West Pakistan, and a freethinking Bangladesh was born as the land of the Bengalis. East Pakistan was gone forever from the territory of Jinnah's Pakistan.

It was the great sacrifice and dedication of our common people that made history in the creation of Bangladesh. From their enormous energy and determination, India got the real motivation to advocate and support the freedom fighters. While the guerrilla war was going on secretly, the anti-Bengali forces became desperate to find the freedom fighters. The Army of West Pakistan was mainly stationed in Dhaka city; they were unfamiliar with the countryside. Thus, the East Pakistani Bengalis, who were enemies of the freedom fighters, got full advantage in all respects.

A few months later, during the period of this civil war, the rainy season arrived, and two-thirds of the country was flooded. The rivers were full of youth with sailing boats travelling noiselessly. People watched the boat race from the riverbanks; everything was great and awesome. Almost eight months passed by and daily life was returning to normal, with some people joining work. The mild winter season came around; the river water went down to its lowest level.

On December 3, 1971, India declared war on Pakistan and directly engaged in military intervention in support of Mukti Bahini (freedom fighters); Pakistan had no choice other than to accept war.

We did not express our slightest gratitude to Indira Gandhi, who boldly supported our struggle for freedom, defying the military superpowers of the world. China was a strong supporter of Pakistan (West). Great Britain which split India in 1947 by pretending that India's minority Muslims would not get fairness from the majority of Hindus. Paradoxically, in 1971, British Christians supported the carnage of the Pakistani minority of Muslims over its majority of Muslims. The USA backed General Yahya's military and arrogantly sent US warships to the Bay of Bengal to threaten Indira. But she simply ignored it.

Ironically, soon after we achieved our victory, instead of thanking Indira, we started making silly excuses against her in favour of Pakistan. Many of us still say that India supported Bangladesh because of its personal interests.

But was it not in the interest of Bangladesh? If India had supported Pakistan like the USA, UK and Islamic countries, what would those Bangladeshis have said then?

The humiliating defeat of Pakistani Punjabis and their Bengali Muslim collaborators who did not want a free Bangladesh could not tolerate that help had been taken from the Hindus' for Bangladesh's independence. So those defeated East Pakistanis said that an independent Bangladesh was not created for the Bengalis but in the interest of the Indians.

Those West Pakistani-loving Bengalis could no longer fight against Mukti Bahini, so after December 16, they rapidly removed their anti-Bengali uniforms and soon turned into a false Mukti Bahini. Shortly, thereafter, they began to show their ungratefulness towards Indira by creating animosity between the people of India and the newly independent Bangladesh.

We should take notes from history and analyse the fact that during the war between India and Pakistan in 1965, India did not attack East Pakistan in her interest. And in

1971 too, they did not occupy and annex East Pakistan as a new state of India. This is a great lesson from India for other civilised countries which waged war against other people and took over their land.

Secondly, after independence, we were again using the poisonous weapons of communalism — saying that it was a shame that the Muslims of Bangladesh did not support a Muslim Zulfiqar, but a Hindu Indira to make Bangladesh a Hindu state.

But who are these Muslims? Obviously, they are the defeated Jinnahist Bengalis, who quickly changed their Pakistani flag and became Bangladesh lovers.

Was Indira a Muslim during our freedom struggle since we loved her so much then? And was Zulfiqar then a Hindu whom we hated? These political Muslims could have then (in 1971) said, "It is a matter of great shame that Pakistani Muslims are killing Pakistani Muslims, so Muslims are fleeing to India to make India a Muslim country."

Even today, we feel ashamed to acknowledge that India provided arms to our Mukti Bahini; we were trained, took refuge, and lived in India for nine months. During those months of atrocities committed by Pakistani Muslims, we (East Pakistanis) had no other place to flee except to Hindu India. Those Pakistani attackers were not only West Pakistani Muslims but also our beloved East Pakistani Muslims, who were very proudly fighting against Mukti Bahini and were extreme enemies of the independence of Bangladesh.

Our first exiled government was formed and operated from West Bengal, India, until the Pakistan Army surrendered. About one-seventh of our population took shelter in India. Indira herself travelled the world to tell them that a baby Bangladesh was born and requested the world leaders to recognise it as a newly independent country. She even talked to powerful world leaders who were against our freedom and was able to earn their recognition for the newborn baby.

All this support and help from Indira Gandhi — we buried in the graveyard just after independence. And yet again, we ungrateful people commenced detesting Indira and India as if our people became desecrated while living as refugees in Hindustan when our Muslims were killing our Muslims.

Who are the in-house enemies in Bangladesh? Who are those who refuse to say Jai Bangla but proudly say that they were freedom fighters? Were there any true freedom fighters in Mukti Bahini who did not roar without saying Jai Bangla? Jai Bangla was the only inspirational word for freedom fighters and Bengali lovers during the guerrilla war. But who are they, who now say Zindabad, and claim to have liberated Bangladesh from Pakistani occupiers?

During the guerrilla war, there was no unified chain of command; there were many different groups with individual leadership in Mukti Bahini. Many of the great warriors of present-day were hiding in the huts of common people; some of them were killing their personal enemies with their 303 rifles. Those who now say that they fought a frontal war against the regular Pakistani Army are liars or Razakars, Al-Badr and Al-Shams who fought against Mukti Bahini and became freedom fighters after December 16, 1971.

Some people now pretend that they were not guerrilla freedom fighters but great soldiers. Actually, they were cowards; when there were no Pakistani and Indian armies in the country, they became such warriors. Indeed, since August 15, 1975, there have been many frontal battles in our free Bangladesh Army.

Since then many patriotic freedom fighters have been killed in the struggle of the armed forces to destroy the true spirit of Bengali freedom fighters. In the process, a military man with his guns finally turned Bangladesh into an Islamic state. Our Mukti Bahini gave birth to a free Bangladesh; but regrettably enough, the Pakistani-minded military brought us back to the old Pakistan except changing its name to the Islamic State of East Pakistan.

To these Islamists of Bangladesh, the surrender of the Pakistani Army to the Indian Army does not exist. Is it not shameful that these blatant liars talk about Islam? In light of this ultra-modern age, how can they distort a historical fact of the world? What did they do in the name of Allah in the Dark Ages? Even Pakistan cannot deny the truth of its surrender to India. If these evil creatures are proud followers of Islam in Bangladesh, then what does Islam mean to them? Will you ever be able to erase the history where a Muslim Yahya (President of Pakistan) surrendered to a Hindu Indira (Prime Minister of India), which was witnessed by the people of this modern world?

Our ex-East Pakistani Bengalis who were brutally fighting and killing Mukti Bahini did not accept the truth because they were and still are anti-Bangladesh; they are very proud to be Muslims. But was Allah with Yahya or with Indira? Who are the actual non-believers who do not believe in religion, or who do not accept the truth? Without admitting the historical truth of our independence, are we not still trying to prove ourselves as an ungrateful nation?

It was only when India declared war on Pakistan on December 3, 1971, and launched airstrikes on the Dacca (Dhaka) cantonment and the runways at Tejgaon Airport and closed the Indian airspace for the West Pakistani Army, that the East Pakistani Army who were still in service with the West Pakistani Army, panicked and fled from the cantonment. Many of them crossed the Buriganga River and reached India via Mawaghat. The ordinary village people provided shelter and all kinds of support to these Bengali army personnel and their families. While they were the real enemies — since they did not look like the West Pakistanis, people helped them flee to India. But what uniform did they wear in India? And after returning after December 16, 1971, what are they wearing in Bangladesh now?

All in all, Indira was the greatest freedom fighter for our free Bengali nation, and she was the woman who liberated Mujib from Bhutto's (Zulfiqar) jail. She arranged the Shimla Agreement between India and Pakistan in 1972, which followed Pakistan's recognition of Bangladesh.

Indira set another great example for the entire world by immediately withdrawing the Indian Army from our newly born Bangladesh in honour of Mujib's demand.

On June 27, 1974, in Dhaka, Mujib welcomed and shook hands with Zulfiqar, who was responsible for that fateful night of March 25, 1971, and caused further bloodshed in the country. But how could the two be friends instantly? It appeared as if nothing had happened between them! Was this not an act of deceiving the people of both countries?

Had the Pakistani Army really killed three million people in nine months, as Mujib claimed. Could he have gone to Lahore (Pakistan) in February 1974 to meet Zulfiqar and Tikka and seek their blessings for Bangladesh's membership in the Organisation of Islamic Cooperation (OIC)?

How could Mujib and Zulfiqar become Islamic friends just after making two nations, while the Muslim pair could not share power in the then single Pakistan? This was historical testimony that clearly stated that what was produced afterwards was just an accident. So, they both brought things back to normal as before — except this time they put the new country into a bottle of old Pakistan.

In 1947, you Indian Muslims went with Jinnah's Pakistan by dividing India to get fairness from your fellow Muslims; thereafter, why could you not live together, you have split yourselves further. Do you need any more self-evident facts that you are cheating yourselves?

Just after two years — we were back to turning it into an Islamic country again. Didn't that warm handshake between the Head of Mukti Bahini and the Chief of Razakar expose that no such real atrocities took place in East Pakistan in those nine months of 1971?

Mujib, who was in jail for over nine months in West Pakistan, probably did not know what was really happening in those months in East Pakistan and what the Bengali patriots had done for his and the country's liberty. He was unexpectedly arrested in Dhaka, after meeting Bhutto and Yahya Khan on the night of March 25 (1971) and was flown to a prison in Punjab. When he was freed, he did not come directly from Lahore to Dhaka or via any neighbouring country, but via London. He went far away from the region to keep Bhutto's wish. As a free man of a free land, Mujib first entered a country that was against our freedom.

Little did he realise how he was freed. Many bootlickers met him and presented him with a new Islamic attar. After taking the helm of the country, Mujib did not try to grasp the difference between a man of speech and a man of responsibility. He did not even try to find out who the patriotic people of our country were. Nawab Siraj-ud-Daulah too, at his time, paid no real attention to his real friends.

Dividing or uniting in the name of religion is simply an ill-motivated leadership to play with the general people.

The majority of Muslims of then Pakistan were East Pakistanis, but no Muslim country in the world had supported us during our struggle for freedom. The Muslim countries of OIC supported the minority Punjabis of West Pakistan and the Razakars, Al-Badrs, and Al-Shams of East Pakistan.

Is it the principle of Islamic religion to support the atrocities of minority Muslims against the majority of Muslims? Muslims perhaps can do such injustice in the name of Islam, but Allah certainly cannot do it if he is believed to be the creator of humankind.

Following the handshakes between Mujib and Bhutto, Mujib brought back the Pakistani Army personnel of the East Bengal regiment, who were serving in West Pakistan even during the liberation war.

We brought them back because they were East Pakistani Muslims; consequently, they joined our newly created Bangladesh Army with promotions. It looked as if servicemen of a country's regular military had been transferred from one unit to another.

Thereafter, in the nightmare of August 15, 1975, the whole spirit of our freedom fighters was viciously murdered along with Mujib's family members by our nearest and dearest Bangladesh Army. It was a well-planned barbaric assassination by cowards in the dark of the night, while people were in deep sleep; even a little child in Mujib's family did not get any mercy from the murderers. In the dark, the army tanks ran into homes of his relatives in the city and killed them too without mercy.

And these tanks were deployed at all important places in Dhaka city to demonstrate the freedom of our Islamic army men to kill the people of free Bengal in the absence of Pakistani and Indian armies.

That freedom we won so easily and that freedom we destroyed instantly. Where were those great (biruttam, birmatdham, birsrastra) forces who pretended that they fought a frontal battle against the Pakistani (West) army when they could not even protect its president in their free country? What were those soldiers slyly doing in the Dhaka cantonment on that night of August 15, 1975? And what did they do afterwards about such unpardonable killings in the history of Pakistan and Bangladesh? And what were those freedom fighters, who say that they have liberated Bangladesh without help from India, doing then?

After the assassination of Bangabandhu (Mujib), many frontal battles were fought against each other's units in the Bangladesh Army. These cold-blooded murderers and liars, subsequently, promulgated the Islamic constitution in Bangladesh.

In this regard, they do not use the word 'Muslim' that the Muslims of Bangladesh are killing the Muslims of Bangladesh to make it Pakistan again. The assassins made Khondaker Mostaq Ahmad sit on the throne for a while, just for eyewash — a few days later, the army men behind the killings extricated Mostaq.

We could very easily differentiate between the Bengali and Punjabi nations because of the physical appearance, so it was very easy to unite us by creating enmity against the West Pakistanis, although we were Muslims on both sides; it was, nonetheless, very hard to do the same among Bengali Muslims as we could easily hide amongst ourselves.

None of our then political leaders, not even any deputy leader, was killed by the Pakistanis (West). The student leaders were the principal force of the Mukti Bahini and great supporters of Mujib, but none of them was killed or even arrested by the Pakistani Army.

Until December 16, 1971, we were all Pakistanis. During our fight for independence, East Pakistani Muslims who were opposed to the anti-Mukti Bahini were telling their beloved West Pakistani brothers that only Hindus and a few Bengali Muslims joined the Mukti Bahini. In 1971, the Hindu community was mostly unjustly persecuted at the hands of anti-Mukti Bahini forces in East Pakistan.

After the world's largest forced mass migrations in 1947, RP Shaha did not move to Bengal in India but stayed in his native Bengal in Pakistan to serve its people. In 1971, he and his son were kidnapped allegedly by the Pakistani Army; their remains were never seen. But which Pakistanis were butchers, East or West?

When Shaha joined the Medical Corps of the Bengal Regiment during the First World War, he was given a gallantry award for saving some British officers from a fire. During our guerrilla war, in the case of patients, the Pakistani Army and Mukti Bahini were provided with equal medical treatment and supplies by Shaha and his Kumudini Hospital. But humanity has few values as compared to religious evils.

Another Hindu, Dhirendranath Dutta, an intellectual politician who struggled to bring an end to British colonial rule, did not go to Indian Bengal but accepted Pakistan as it was his native home. He became a lawmaker of the Constituent Assembly of the new state (Pakistan); when Urdu was imposed as the only state language of Pakistan, he defended the Bengali language in the assembly in 1948.

It was our great shame, being born as Bengalis, that not a single Bengali Muslim politician rose in the assembly to support his proposal. In 1971, in the eyes of the army, every Hindu was considered a traitor to Pakistan. The eighty-five-year-old Dutta was abducted along with his young son and murdered like RP Shaha and his son by the Islamic Republic of Pakistan.

Now, in free Bangladesh where the Bengalis of the Hindu community should be highly respected, Hindus are once again being victimised simply because of their religious belief. But we, perhaps, will never realise that Bangladesh is first their country, then ours. If we are associated with Islam, is it our religious character to abhor Allah's other creatures? Yes, it really is; the historic evidence of our acts confirms this.

Patriotic freedom fighters joined the Mukti Bahini on that horrifying night of March 25, 1971 — for their motherland — and they returned to their own business on December 16, 1971, as their mission to give birth to a free Bangladesh ended that day.

Many of them probably never sought any benefit from the state; maybe they said, "We have not liberated our poor country for our personal gain; it is time to rebuild it, for which it has been set free."

At least some patriotic freedom fighters did not even expose themselves as freedom fighters, and they never went to the authorities to seek their certificates — because they were ashamed when they saw that many of those who were receiving certificates for being great fighters, were not freedom fighters at all.

Many of the real leading freedom fighters did not know then that furious Pakistani soldiers had surrendered to the Indians at our Ramna Racecourse Maydan; not many believed that such a surrender really happened, as the city was almost empty after Indian airstrikes and bombings around Dhaka cantonment and Tejgaon Airport, which continued day and night.

At that time, we were living near Rampura TV station as my father had sold his house at 93 Aga Sadek Road. At the TV station and also behind it, was an open field where the army had built a huge camp, from where they patrolled regularly.

I remember the siren sounding one night; people rushing into nearby trenches; on a blackout night, a few minutes later, the sky lit up with a ball of fire like scattered stars. High in the sky, a couple of birds seemed to be flying, but at night!

A series of rays could be seen emanating from the cantonment seconds after; they were air strikes, maybe Indian fighter planes had arrived.

How had those Indians dared to enter our country's airspace, fly over Dhaka, and carried out attacks on the ferocious Pakistani Army?

Moments later, something like a fish-catching bird started descending rapidly; now it was quite clear that a fighter jet had turned upwards after dropping something on the ground in the airport area. Shortly thereafter, a large cloud of dust could be seen rising into the air.

The next day, there were similar scenes but during the day; and they were frequent. Each scene was thrilling and unique. It was like a cockfight in the sky between the Indian Hunter and MIG fighters versus Pakistani Sabre jets. They were flying overhead; the pilots were clearly seen sitting in their cockpits and firing at the enemy aircraft.

I remember that a Sabre jet came around and ran after a Hunter fighter; a Pakistani (Bengali or Punjabi) pilot was shaking his head as if he was about to catch the enemy fighter. At some point, the Hunter was hit; it caught fire and escaped at maximum speed, likely falling there.

Oh, yeah; but by then it may have reached the Indian airspace.

Since our country is surrounded by India from all sides, it takes only a few minutes for them to come and go.

A few days later, only Indian fighter jets were seen over the city, and they dominated the sky of East Pakistan. There was no more cockfight; no anti-aircraft shots were fired.

Only those who were still in Dacca (Dhaka) city and came out of their homes saw how the Indian Army was escorting the Pakistani Army on foot from the cantonment along the Airport Road as prisoners of war (POWs).

Subsequently, when people came to know of this, many freedom fighters of the present time started entering the new country. A surrendering ceremony was arranged between Pakistani and Indian armies in the open field of our Ramna Racecourse Maydan, but none of our great (birsrastra …) fighters was there. Where were they actually at the time? How had the enemies left Bangladesh without the knowledge of our great frontal-war warriors?

And where had the East Pakistani Muslim soldiers and agents, who were fighting enthusiastically against Mukti Bahini alongside the West Pakistani Army, gone? Had they fled from Bangladesh to Pakistan? Of course not; actually, they are now enjoying the most in a free Bangladesh. Since these Bengali soldiers did not look like West Pakistanis despite being Muslims, the Indian Army did not take them as POWs.

By surrendering, General Niazi saved lots of lives.

After the surrender, anyone could have become a freedom fighter in free Bangladesh, such as mushrooms growing in the wild. Then, we cowardly killed many innocent Biharis and threw their bodies into the rivers, whereas we do not know how the entire Pakistani army left Bangladesh.

And then, we began looting and grabbing properties — from industries to forests, hills, cotton mills to jute mills … Eventually, we managed to completely digest all nuts, bolts, and everything of Adamjee Jute Mills — at the time when it was part of Pakistan, it was our biggest source of employment and the largest jute mill in the world, established in the river port town of Narayanganj.

If we can be so proud as freedom fighters, we must be ashamed of what we have been doing and are still doing against our country since independence. We fought for only nine months, but how long will we take advantage of it?

And those who are fake freedom fighters and enjoying all the privileges at the cost of others, which religion do they believe in? What kind of punishment have they received from their religious organisation? Doesn't their conscience prick them?

## 3.2 Never had Pakistan occupied our land but had occupied our mother tongue.

The West Pakistanis were not as bad as we used to say at Paltan Maydan in 1968-69. Nor were they the occupiers of our country, as we say today.

I was then a student of classes 8 and 9 of Nabakumar Institute. Paltan Maydan was one of my playgrounds as it was near my parent' home on Aga Sadek Road. All the big sports competitions were held at Dhaka Stadium, where I used to enjoy them regularly. I used to attend almost every meeting of any political party held at Paltan Maydan in those days. I just listened to the politicians and saw what people were doing; I participated in many demonstrations to observe what was happening there. One day, President Ayub Khan humbly stepped down from power.

Mujib was the main accused in the Agartala Conspiracy Case and was arrested in 1968; some months later, when it was announced that he was going to be released from Dhaka cantonment jail, the streets of the city from Chandkharpul and Curzon Hall area to Tejgaon Airport became a hotbed of turmoil, as a large crowd gathered to see who Mujib was. From that day, he suddenly became so popular in East Pakistan that all the other prominent politicians of the province significantly lost their political voices. Later, in the election of Yahya (December 1970), Mujib won with an overwhelming majority.

General Ayub Khan came to power in a bloodless coup d'état in October 1958. He reigned in good faith during a very critical period in Pakistan. The period of industrialisation that took place during his tenure was regarded as a 'great decade' in the history of the country. He built many infrastructure projects, including canals, dams and power plants; he was credited with making the country one of Asia's fastest-growing economies. But he was criticised mainly for beginning the first of the army's incursions into civilian politics.

He made Dhaka the second capital of Pakistan. Many remarkable public institutions, schools and colleges were constructed during his time — the Kamalapur railway station, High Court that is now our Supreme Court (moving the zoo to Mirpur), Sangsad Vaban (the parliament), Karmitola International Airport — though its terminal was yet to be completed, as he resigned after the students' uprising and handed over power to General Yahya in March 1969. Much of his good work and planning are still visible in our country.

You cannot randomly deny someone's good work just because he was a military man. Time witnessed that Ayub and the other military rulers of Pakistan and present-day Bangladesh were not at all people of the same category. We may not give him credit for his work, but somebody else cannot certainly take credit for the work that Ayub has done.

He introduced a 'basic democracy' in a country where most people still do not know whom to vote for, why they need to vote, and the values of voting. The people of his national and provincial cabinets were highly skilled and efficient. Under his strict rules and excellent discipline, the general people as well as ethnic and religious vulnerable communities were better protected, and they enjoyed more freedom than in today's Bangladesh.

We may be offended by what our fellow Pakistani brothers have done against us, but we cannot be angry at what they have not done against us. Other people around the world have struggled for freedom for years and centuries. We do not need to show our fight as a super heavyweight liberation war through falsehood.

If we speak our minds now, Pakistan will not come to take our country back. The very important criteria for judging West Pakistanis were that they attacked our mother tongue and forced us to speak Urdu even though we were a majority. Secondly, they did not give us overall autonomy, still, we never wanted a separation. Thirdly, they refused to give power to Bengalis even though we won the general elections in Pakistan under their government. These three key issues were enough to break our ties with them.

Look at us now, we have made a Dhaka-centric country where the city has become a hell to live in. Why are we so cruel to our comrades in the Chittagong Hill Tracts? Why have we ignored their autonomy since independence and the fundamental rights of indigenous people elsewhere in the country? Is it because they are minorities, weak and naïve, so élite religio-politicians can grab their land? Their lust for this is a clear sign of an increase in the percentage of the majority religious population. It is very interesting to observe the correlation between increasing religiosity and increasing corruption in the country.

The agony our indigenous people have been suffering for a long time is no less than the pain we suffered at the hands of Pakistan. The so-called minorities and indigenous people are citizens of Bangladesh just like us and they should enjoy the same rights as our top religious leaders.

Forced eviction from their ancestral lands and exploitation by the capitalist classes in the name of development made most of the Santal population homeless and landless; on the other hand, money lenders exploited their poverty. The colonial British laws have now made the indigenous communities encroachers on their own land in Bangladesh.

No human in the world can be illegal. But the rule of law can make it happen. It is an unjust law. We, the state, continue to exploit indigenous peoples, annihilate their history, and deny them their authentic rights. These vulnerable people face various types of discrimination while land grabbers are becoming more and more desperate to occupy the lands of native people in the absence of justice in Bangladesh, and false promises are made by our government just to let their revolts die down.

A series of random killings in the armed forces and the political and religious madness among the opponents are extremely tragic; many death monuments could have been built in the country, but none has been built. Why? If we look at Pakistanis, they allowed us to build the Shaheed Minar.

In 2006, the political frenzy reached the height of anarchy in Bangladesh's history. Passenger-laden trains and buses were set on fire to grab power. People killed people as if they were in an amusement park for murder! Horrifying scenes were seen everywhere like a killing feast between two political opponents; supporters of one adversary party were dancing on the bodies of another group.

## 3.3 How many days did our British-arranged marriage with Pakistan exist? When Urdu was imposed as the only state language of Pakistan, what role did our Bengali Muslim leaders play?

The truth is that Pakistan never occupied our land; while in 1947, some Indian Bengali Muslim leaders ignored the common people and ran after Mohammed Ali Jinnah and created Pakistan from India. Jinnah was neither a man of the people nor a man of religion. But he was able to become the father of a newly formed Muslim nation. What kind of religious morality did the Muslim leaders of Indian Bengal have when they abandoned their mother tongue and went to live in Jinnah's home? Nor did they follow the path of their fellow Mawlana Azad, who was an active follower of Mahatma Gandhi and firmly opposed the division of India on religious bloodlines.

In 1947, the incompetent politicians of East Bengal did not join Azad, but instead went to the other end of India to make our new home with Sindhi, Balochi, Pathan and Punjabi Muslims, whose language we did not understand, nor did they understand ours. A country whose two wings were separated by more than 1,800 kilometres of Indian Territory. We had nothing in common but a Muslim identity.

How long did that British-arranged marriage exist? Right after our happy marriage, Jinnah made Urdu the only state language of Pakistan. Just after making a new home with our dearest religious brothers and sisters, the people of East Bengal lost their freedom to speak in their mother tongue.

On February 25, 1948, when Pakistan was barely six months old, Dhirendranath Dutta, a legislator from East Bengal in the Constituent Assembly of the new state (Pakistan), tabled an amendment in the parliament demanding that the Bengali language be adopted as a medium of expression along with English and Urdu. Pakistan Governor General Jinnah was presiding over the session.

Dutta argued, "Out of six crores and ninety lakhs of people inhabiting this state, four crores and forty lakhs of people speak the Bengali language. So, sir, what should be the state language? The state language should be the language which is used by majority of the people of the State, and for that, sir, I consider that the Bengali language is a lingua franca of our State."

The leaders of the most abused and persecuted minority community of Pakistan spoke in a very hostile environment in defence of the mother tongue of all the people of East Bengal.

Dutta's statement was supported by another lawmaker, Prem Hari Barma, "Sir, this amendment does not seek to oust English or Urdu altogether, but it seeks only to have Bengali as one of the media spoken in the Assembly by the Members of the Assembly."

Prime Minister Nawabzada Liaquat Ali Khan rose to say, "He (Dutta) should realise that Pakistan has been created because of the demand of a hundred million Muslims in this subcontinent and the language of a hundred million Muslims is Urdu; and, therefore, it is wrong for him now to try and create the situation that as the majority of the people of Pakistan belong to one part of Pakistan, the language which is spoken there should become the state language of Pakistan. I have never heard in the central assembly for years and years any voice raised by the people of Bengal that Bengali should be the State language. Urdu can be the only language which can keep the people of East Bengal or the Eastern Zone and the people of the Western Zone joined together. A nation must have one language and that language can only be Urdu and no other language."

I wonder how this prime minister could argue so slyly in favour of the Urdu language, where no single language is considered common to the whole population of Pakistan even after the separation of East Bengal (Bangladesh). Their mother tongues are mainly Punjabi, Sindhi, Pashto and Balochi. Urdu is the primary language of the Muslims of northern India. Only a small fraction of Pakistan's élite population speaks Urdu. It is the youngest and not the indigenous language of any province in Pakistan but has ideological significance in Pakistani politics.

Thus, how could this Nawabzada say just six months after its creation that Pakistan was created because of the demand of a hundred million Muslims of the Indian subcontinent and the language of those hundred million Muslims was Urdu? And how could all those Bengali Muslim leaders in the assembly support this blundering argument of the prime minister? Was this their special quality and morality as Muslim lawmakers?

Secondly, Muslims were a minority in undivided India. How could some of those minorities have demanded a separate state under the guise of religion? Thirdly, the people of India were not asked to vote for the creation of Pakistan. So, did Prime Minister Khan's argument in favour of Urdu have any factual basis, which, in fact, was the least spoken language in the country?

As a spoken language, Urdu was originally derived from Hindustani, which is the lingua franca of the region between the Ganges and Jamuna rivers near Delhi; instead of the Hindi alphabet, Urdu is written in the Arabic-Persian alphabet to give it a Muslim flavour to Hindustani. But when you hear the articulation of Urdu, it is indeed, a dialect of Hindi, which has some Islamic words in it.

Bengali-speaking Pakistanis were the majority of the whole of Pakistan as the population of East Bengal province was more than the other four provinces of Pakistan. So, instead of fooling himself, the prime minister could perhaps better argue that since only a few Urdu-speaking élite Muslim leaders of India created Pakistan just six months ago, Arabic must be the only state language of Pakistan.

However, when he sat down, Bhupendra Kumar Dutta, another member of the Constituent Assembly of Pakistan (CAP) from East Bengal, took the floor, "Sir, we press this amendment in no frivolous spirit of opposition. I am surprised at the speech the Honourable Leader of the House has just made. I wish he had not made some of the remarks he chose to make. They will have unfortunate repercussions elsewhere even in certain sections of Pakistan. Therefore, it is all the more necessary that this amendment should be passed."

After a flood of interruptions from other members, Bhupendra continued, "But here we are adopting Urdu. Urdu is not the language of any of the provinces constituting the dominion of Pakistan. It is the language of the upper few of western Pakistan. This opposition to the amendment proves an effort, a determined effort on the part of the upper few of western Pakistan to dominate the state of Pakistan."

This was followed by East Bengal Chief Minister Khwaja Nazimuddin, among others, who maliciously conceived an anti-Bengal rhetoric and strongly opposed Dhirendranath's amendment.

The motion was rejected.

It was only members of the Hindu community (CAP) who wholeheartedly accepted Dhirendranath Dutta's proposal on February 25, 1948. Unfortunately, no Muslim CAP member adopted Bengali as one of their official languages. Not a single Bengali-speaking Muslim legislator supported this motion.

It showed once again the characteristics of those Bengali Muslim leaders who chased Jinnah in 1947, giving up their language and cultural identity. Ironically, they were and still are highly respected as national heroes in free Bangladesh. Is this not political criminality in the name of religious majority?

The untenable characterisation of 'Bengali' by Nawabzada Liaquat Ali Khan and his anti-Bengali cohorts was challenged only by members of the Hindu community on the CAP floor, for all Bengali-speaking people. But do we ever remember them? How many people in Bangladesh know the name of Dhirendranath Dutta?

Any deliberate injustice has an adverse effect on itself as well. Even Liaquat Ali Khan, Khwaja Nazimuddin, and their associates knew that what they had done as Muslims in the central legislature was totally irrational and wrong. But history repeats itself, perhaps because we often forget to learn any lessons from it.

The outright rejection of Dhirendranath's pro-Bengali amendment had a serious impact on the student community and intelligentsia of East Bengal. About its repercussions — four years later, the general people of East Bengal set a great example for their Muslim leadership, who falsely used religion to deceive people. As a result, on February 21, 1952, the support for the Bengali language became historic evidence for the country.

Those Muslim leaders of East Bengal were, in fact, an integral part of taking away the basic right of the people to speak Bengali and forcing them to speak in Urdu. Look at those religious brokers over and over again — even after the historic Bengali language movement in 1952, the provincial name of East Bengal was purposefully erased and renamed East Pakistan in 1955. With this step, they hurt not only the heart of our mother tongue but also the heart of our historic land, 'Bengal'.

Having said all this, is it not clear, as per law, that a legitimate Pakistan was created on August 14, 1947, with our consent? We cannot, therefore, lie today by saying that Pakistan was an occupying force. We must not forget that we were also Pakistanis till December 16, 1971; East Pakistan was their land, and West Pakistan was ours, as we were both born under the same religious umbrella at the same time. They did not come to us; we ran after them. And every day, we sang our national anthem with great respect: paak sarzameen shaad baad … until March 25, 1971.

So, in this regard, those who supported Pakistan during the Bengalis' liberation war cannot be considered as anti-Bangladesh. They had every right to protect the sovereignty of the two wings of Pakistan. Many Bengali parents supported Pakistani forces, while their children supported Mukti Bahini and vice versa.

But the anti-Mukti Bahini forces (Razakars, Al-Badrs, Al-Shams, etc.) who deliberately committed serious crimes by being soldiers of Allah and who are yet to accept Bangladesh as their home, are the real culprits. In 1971 they used to say, "Mukti Bahini is created by Hindus, and Mujib is a Hindu too; so, fight hard against Mukti Bahini."

Some Muslim leaders in undivided India pretended that they would not get justification from the majority of Hindus. Do they now ask themselves what fairness their other Muslim communities in Pakistan have got from them?

When the Arab-Persian-Mughal Muslims ruled India as outsiders, was it not a question of fairness and justice for Hindus in their own land? Bengali Muslims have no answer to this question because they did not exist then.

Religious, non-religious, and indigenous Indians had long fought against the tyrannical Christians in one voice; Jinnah was also one of them. But why did he finally leave the Indian stage and kiss Mountbatten for his Muslim identity?

He could instead have gone to a middle eastern country near India or with Mountbatten, who would have guaranteed him that he could practise Islam in England.

Jinnah became the father of the nation of Pakistan, i.e., the father of the Bengali, Bihari, Punjabi, Sindhi, and Baluchi nations; but all these jatis (nations), existed long before Jinnah's great-grandfather was born.

We Bengalis regarded him as the father of the nation with utmost gratitude and always respected him; no political party ever treated him disrespectfully. But just after 1971, we erased his name from everywhere in Bangladesh as if Jinnah did not ever exist in our country's history.

After the partition, Biharis came from India to Pakistan (East Bengal) because they were Muslim by religion, so as a principle of division they chose this eastern part of Pakistan to settle down, which was the nearest, and became Pakistani. Many of them owned most of the business entities on Nawabpur Road in Dhaka. After this part of Pakistan became Bangladesh, the government did not recognise them as Bangladeshis but rather as Pakistanis; and since then they have been kept in refugee camps in a miserable condition.

Is it not sheer hypocrisy? Biharis and Bengalis were the same citizens of Pakistan for twenty-four years; the only difference was that they were from Bihar and spoke Urdu; many Bengali Muslims also came here from Bihar and other states of India; however, we have rendered Biharis homeless in their own land. No government in Bangladesh accepted them as Bangladeshis even though they were not West Pakistanis. Like these government officials of Bangladesh, they were also the same citizens of Pakistan.

Aren't these religio-politicians just a bunch of scoundrels? How inhuman they are to their own Muslims, but when Muslims are badly treated in someone else's house, they come out too loudly to show sympathy for them. Can you believe what a religious game this is? How could we reject Biharis who were here for the same reason as us? Otherwise, this part of Pakistan would have remained Indian Bengal.

Bangladesh literally means the Land of Bengal. It is predominately an agricultural country. The vast majority of the population directly depends on their fertile soils, which are exceptionally rich as deltaic regions. Much of the country was formed by the alluvial plains of the Ganges and Brahmaputra river systems, originating from the Himalayas and discharging into the Bay of Bengal. Bengal is located on the delta in the northeastern part of the Indian subcontinent.

It is a great landmass of South Asia, which is home to one of the world's oldest civilisations. The subcontinent comprises the territory of present-day India, Pakistan, Bangladesh, Nepal, Sri Lanka, Bhutan and Maldives.

Topographically, Bangladesh is a low-lying area. The lifestyle of most populations is very similar, as they live and depend on their tropical natural environment. The Bengal plains — the largest delta in the world — were gradually built by tidal deposits carried out by many rivers and streams. Floods and cyclones are seasonal features, which are to a large extent due to the geographical location and natural drainage system. The Indian state of Assam, which borders the northeastern part of Bangladesh, receives the highest rainfall in the world. People live happily in normal floods, though unusual ones make their lives very difficult. However, the country is naturally cleaned by floodwater once a year; and it brings sediments, which are most essential for seasonal crops.

Bangladesh is surrounded by India from all sides except a short frontier with Myanmar (Burma) on the far south-eastern side of the Bay of Bengal. Together with the Indian state of West Bengal, it makes up the ethnolinguistic region of Bengal. The borders of the region that constitute present-day Bangladesh were established in 1947 by the greatest partition and tragedy experienced by humankind. The eastern part of Bengal became the eastern part of Pakistan. No land frontier existed between the two ex-wings of Pakistan. Indeed, the immense territory of India remains between the two.

A land, whatever name is given to it, is always known by its geographical location with its native inhabitants, culture, and history. A country's people can be transformed and moved to another place, but its landmass cannot be moved.

Our unique identity is that we are Bengalis; this is our great inspiration to be a unique nation. We fought for it as our original identity was denied during the rule of West Pakistan. We must vigorously and tangibly reject religious identity in society. Religion is a totally personal matter. No man has the right to impose divine orders on others.

Being an independent country, it is very unfortunate that we could not build a true cultural bridge between the two Bengals. It is a pity that we live like each other's constant enemies while we speak the same language and share the same soil, the same water, and the same air. There is not much that Individuals or groups of individuals can do about this unless goodwill is involved by both governments. We are very proud of ourselves, but many of us are unaware of our true cultural values. As a country, Bangladesh may have been born only in 1971, but the ethnic identity of its people has been in existence much longer.

Political parties may have different manifestos for the sake of politics, but we all have at least one vital thing in common, i.e., our distinct cultures and traditions. The identity of our geographical origin in this world is also very significant. Thus, all political parties must set the country's true geo-cultural heritage at the top of their political agenda. This may help people integrate with their fundamental issues irrespective of other things.

It could also help strengthen the political foundation of the nation. And then, whichever political party it is or whoever rules the country, they will not hesitate to give the utmost respect to the people, where all diversified ethnic people are an integral part.

## 3.4 The two-nation conspiracy theory of British Christian occupiers under the guise of religion to split India.

Pakistan was created by the British conspirators who pretended that India's minority Muslims would not be treated fairly by the majority Hindus.

The historic evidence of the British conspiracy is crystal clear. You should simply ask yourselves what justification Muslims got from each other after creating a Muslim nation. Why is it that its own Bengali, Bihari, Punjabi, and other Muslim communities are badly treated by its other Muslim communities?

If Muslims could not live with Hindus, then Pakistan should have been home to all Muslims in India. But there are still more Muslims living delightfully in India than in Pakistan. Pakistani Muslims from East and West too had been living in India for hundreds of years, but why couldn't they live together in their own Islamic country? Muslim separatists might have regretted the two-nation religious theory, but have those British Christians ever regretted it?

Do Muslims who are still living in India have the right to live in Pakistan? According to the theory, the answer is 'yes'. But will Pakistan accept them as its citizens?

If they do not, what was the justification of the British Christians' two-nation theory, which triggered the greatest forced migration and suffering of the innocents in the history of humankind? Millions died, and millions had to permanently abandon their indigenous homes and properties to become refugees in other people's homes.

Did this act of British cruelty not create more minorities in both countries than in undivided India alone? Aren't the minorities in India and Pakistan more vulnerable after the partition? Was this not an act of extreme inhumanity deliberately inflicted by the Christian occupiers in India?

Did any World Tribunal hang these vicious criminals?

In India, not only Muslims but many other religious minority groups also lived; why did the English not create a separate homeland for each of them? Why did they choose only the Muslim minority?

By their religious theory, will they divide Great Britain for its religious minorities? If British Protestants were the sons of god, then for the sake of righteousness, why did they not divide the entire world into separate homelands for each religion?

Not only as invaders but also as the least minority, on what religious principles did they persecute all the majority religious communities in the Indian subcontinent?

Hindus and Muslims were living side by side in harmony in India, though differences existed within the same religion too. The British Christians made many evil plans to split Hindu-Muslim unity and recruited traitors from society.

Along with their nefarious designs behind the partition, they were able to cover up nearly two hundred years of genocide against the people of the subcontinent.

Instead of using the term Indians for an incident that took place, they often deliberately used Hindu and Muslim, to stoke it as a political issue. Even in the 21$^{st}$ century, for any news about Iraq they use the words, Shia and Sunni, just to incite religious schism in other parts of the world; although, on a similar issue about themselves, they do not use the terms Catholic and Protestant. How could they drive the Palestinians out of their own homeland and create Israel?

They talk about the world of democracy, but they have ruled India autocratically for two long centuries; and never did they talk about a democratic India during their long occupation. Even when they partitioned India, they did not ask its people; instead, they chose a few self-styled Muslim leaders to fulfil their real intention.

Before they took over India, Britons bribed Mir Jafar; when they had to leave, they chose Jinnah to destroy the unity and great power of India. Second, they intentionally left some issues unresolved so that India and Pakistan would become perpetual enemies of each other. Third, while the people of India and Pakistan would be fighting against each other, they would not recall the British barbarism in India and would soon forget who their real enemies were.

## 3.5 Were civilised people born before indigenous people? Where did civilised people actually come from?

The arrogance of some civilised people tells us that they were born earlier than primitive people and were always born in a civilised dress.

Nature blossoms anew each time in a great diversity but never gives up its originality. Every rich person in this modern world is always born naked like in the Stone Age. And when they die, though their corpse is beautifully decorated, this distinction in prosperity vanishes as soon as the insects descend upon the body.

In the last 200 years, scientists have concluded that humans have only lived on the earth for a short period of its history. They believe the earth is about 4.6 billion years old. This estimate is based on radiometric age dating. Certain elements emit energy; this is called radioactivity. Over time, the elements cause radioactivity to decay. If an object has a half-life of one million years, half of the element causing radioactivity will decay over a period of one million years. Radiometric age dating is not precise, but it does provide us with a vague estimate of the age of the earth.

A dead body was found inside a house in the western world a few days ago; the police believed (estimated) the body was already a few weeks old as it had started to decay and was covered with insects. In those weeks, possibly from earlier, the children, grandchildren, and neighbours of the deceased woman were unaware of what had happened to the 92-year-old living alone; however, they all knew what was happening then in the powerhouse of the world.

We know a great deal about what will happen to our dead bodies in an empty space in hell; however, we do not know what is going on in our neighbour's house.

History began when humans learned to read and write. The first writing we know of came from the civilisations of Mesopotamia and Egypt about 5,500 years ago. People had lived for thousands of years before this, but little had changed from generation to generation. They lived as nomads. Nomads are people who have no permanent home. Men hunted animals, and women gathered wild plants. When there were no more animals to hunt or plants to gather, they moved to a new place.

Primitive people did not acquire knowledge by reading books. Knowledge is innately acquired from one's mind by looking at nature and the experiences gathered along with it. Prehistoric humans lived for millennia in the Stone Age before they knew writing; they passed their experience from generation to generation, which made the knowledge of indigenous people unique in their respective geographical regions.

Even in this modern time, we have not really understood the indigenous peoples and their rich knowledge, but we know how to root out their true history and how to write new history about the 'New World' in the name of god. As we civilised people are mostly materialists, we probably think that indigenous people are living in hell. So, we go to teach them that they will like our way of life. Even in advanced technocratic countries, poverty persists miserably. Natural, free-minded people do not want to live in such a strange way. They are better off being poor in their rich natural environment.

If you put some birds with tons of delicious food in a nice cosy cage, the birds will never stay in it; they know what freedom really is.

In prehistoric times, people were neither poor nor rich; any sensible person of this modern era can easily see that. The words rich and poor might not have existed when the earth was purely natural and owned by aboriginal people. In terms of money, it was the richest time on this earth. Wasn't it?

Society evolved while people began doing individual jobs. This is called 'division of labour'. The division of labour caused people to depend on one another and eventually led to an advanced civilisation, as we call it.

## 3.6 European hungry pirates robbed the nautical routes of the Indian Ocean in the late 15th century.

For several centuries, the countries of Europe had heard fabulous stories about India and dreamt of conquering it. Alexander conquered the whole civilised world, stopping short of India because his men on horseback refused to go further to encounter the men on elephants whom they had never met before. He then set up a pillar and declared it the farthest end of the civilised world.

The world continued to hear about India's wealth and continued to invade it from the north — the land route lay by that side — with the object of plunder and, in some cases, to rule and establish dynasties.

The people who came to India to trade were Arabs and the Chinese. They were looking for spices, raw cotton, silk and gems. In return, they were to barter or sell their products here.

The neighbours of the Indus Valley exchanged their mathematical knowledge at the beginning of the first century from person to person and across generations. The number zero '0' which is nothing, the infinity '∞' which is superior to any number, and the 'decimal' system were invented by Indian mathematicians. The Hindu numeral system was adopted by the Arabs, and later, they transmitted the system to Europeans.

At the time while Europeans were keen to trade with Hindus and the people of the Far East, it was not safe for Christians to reach India through the land route of the vast territories of the Ottoman (Turkish) Empire. Therefore, their long dreams depended only on their destiny to reach India and whether they could sail to an unknown destination.

It was assumed that the earth was flat — it was normal to have such an idea — but that is what the sacred books of God say. After a desperate sailing boat journey in 1492, Christopher Columbus's wooden boat, propelled by the sails and his men, reached a land whose people he called native Indians; he was sure and insisted that he had arrived in India.

In fact, he had reached the continent of America whose existence was not known at all to Europeans. So, he discovered it and named it the 'New World' America. How could history be written in such a way that Columbus (a Catholic) discovered America when many native people were living there long before the arrival of Europeans? These indigenous Americans lived naked like other animals; was that why white Christians did not recognise them as human beings? Who discovered Europe? Someone from another continent surely came to Europe first. If they did not know that person, how could their Bible know that Adam was the first man on earth?

Six years later, in 1498, after a very long risky sea voyage, a Portuguese sailor named Vasco da Gama finally managed to anchor his sailing boat to a busy port in India. Gama was surprised to see the extensive trading opportunities there. He kept the nautical route a secret from other Europeans. Much later, i.e., more than half a century later, the mystery was eventually leaked to their rivals — the Dutch and English pirates.

In 1510, the Portuguese invaded Sultan Yousuf Shah of Bijapur and established their rule over Goa by annexing the Indian province as Portuguese India. It remained their colony until India recaptured it in 1961.

Following the nautical routes of Portuguese Catholics to reach India from Europe, by the mid-16$^{th}$ century, Dutch Protestants were finally able to sail for the Indian Ocean with some experienced pirates on boats.

The pirates of the English islanders were a bit late in the race to seize this new fortune but were very wary and not in a hurry; yet, for a long period, they had been spying on Portuguese boats and planning secret strategies to intervene. Meanwhile, they (English Protestants) were too busy following the Spanish sea route to reach the goldmines of natives or natural Americans. They had already intercepted the Spanish pirates' boats, which were full of gold, on the way back to Spain.

Catholics and Protestants fought internally against each other to establish their supremacy over the golden sea routes of the 'New World' America, yet because of their common beliefs, they shared the wealth of others amongst themselves and randomly killed many of America's innocent aborigines. They systematically destroyed the birthplace of the great, ancient Maya civilisation in order to completely eradicate it from the history of the old world — which was full of rich natural resources from which tons of gold and other valuables were looted.

By this time, the English islanders were able to establish their supremacy by sending triple-masted sailing boats to other parts of the so-called New World, and then, they eyed India.

The French could not make any significant influence on the Indian subcontinent, but they sailed to catch the winds of Africa. Later, these two historically rival countries fought for several centuries to occupy the occupied territories and capture new territories of other peoples.

In the first half of the 16th century, the nautical routes along India's west coast near the Arabian Sea in the Indian Ocean were dominated by the Portuguese, who effectively blocked any boats of other European countries. Dutch Protestants, on the other hand, fought to gain control of the sea route from the Portuguese Catholics.

Meanwhile, in 1526, ambitious Babur — with his shining sword — ventured into India through the Hindu Kush Mountains from Afghanistan to establish his kingdom in Delhi, thereby laying the foundation of the Mughal Empire in Hindustan.

In the latter half of the 16th century, the Portuguese began to fade. The Englishmen were closely monitoring the situation. For decades, they had been spying on the Portuguese sites to possess nautical maps to go to India. When they finally succeeded, they sailed towards an unknown destination. They were constantly on watch duty after anchoring a coastline in the Indian Ocean. Initially, they were interested in the spice trade in the Far East; Java was their potential trade post. But the Dutch had already established a stronghold there, so the English mission ended in complete failure. Then they turned their gaze towards India.

The 16th century was very painful and a dismal failure for the English pirates off the coast of India. Constant skirmishes with the mightier Portuguese resulted in many defeats and losses. Some brave Englishmen defied the Portuguese blockade, but they were merely pirates, killing and looting their foes without mercy. On the other hand, cooperation between the English and Dutch Protestants against the Portuguese Catholics worked for some time to control the Spice Islands of Java and the Far East.

Some individual Englishmen acted as spies for others and penetrated the soil of the Indian subcontinent as spice brokers. Rivals grew for the monopoly of trade among them. Some of them tried to form a company to vie effectively with their competitors. In the non-industrialised world at that time, the spice trade from this part of Asia to Europe was highly profitable.

Nearly a century of Catholic monopoly in the Indian Ocean was about to be taken over by their Protestant foes.

From the beginning of the 17$^{th}$ century, English spice traders began to show up as the only monopolists in the vast market of the subcontinent. Owing to the generosity and blessings of the Mughal emperors, John, an English merchant, started to build factories (a sort of cantonment) in the port cities of Madras and Bombay. Initially, they were trading in spices in the name of John Company (which later became the East India Company) without paying duty; they gradually shifted to textiles — especially the light-patterned cotton characteristic of Bengal.

And finally, they came closer to the Bay of Bengal on the banks of the Hugli River in Calcutta (Kolkata) in search of more fortune in greater India. In this prosperous province, Bengal, around the end of the 17$^{th}$ century, John's East India Company firmly established its strong base by the grace of Emperor Aurangzeb.

That was how Europeans entered India — a magnificent land of forests, rivers, animals, birds, and lots more.

During the natural world, i.e., before the invention of engines or motors, from the 15$^{th}$ century onwards, starving pirates from European countries came to the shores of Indian seaports in their sailing boats to rob from these areas, and they gradually established their presence in India as spice traders. After settling comfortably in the country, they cunningly converted Indians, mainly Hindus and Muslims, into Christianity.

In every civilised human society, they have upper and lower classes of people, though they have not defined the system that way. In Hindu society, however, it has been clearly stated according to their profession. Thus, by taking advantage of the caste system in Hinduism, Christianity fraudulently and immorally converted lower-class Hindus more easily into Christians.

Slowly, they introduced the Portuguese Catholic Church, English Protestant Church and other churches in the name of their respective gods. And they were the princes of God. Hence, they had the divine mandate to occupy the countries of other peoples — those which were not created by their God. Then they oppressed the people and kept them as their slaves for enjoyment. Many of these Europeans subsequently embraced Islam in India to get the benefit of having several women as their wives. English Christians also came to Hindustan to hunt and earn their bread and butter.

The original purpose of their long and harsh sailing boat journey might have been to proselytise or act as spice merchants, but many of them were lured by India. Many others entered servitude with many kings, especially in the Deccan. They worked as soldiers, advisers or mercenaries. Some of them were completely Indianized, wearing Indian clothes and eating Indian curry. Over the decades, they had found that life in India had offered them far more than they could have expected at home. They could not have such luxuries, servants, slaves and all the rest in their homeland. Thus, they had no intention of returning to England.

The English pirates, who were notorious for not bathing daily, were introduced to the concept of shampoo by their Indian consorts, and this habit was carried back to England, where the men who bathed every day were ridiculed by the locals. Many of the Englishmen who lived some distance away from the main cities of Madras, Bombay and Calcutta were lured to the Indian way of life. Apostasy was a serious concern in England among the lords of the East India Company.

The early Europeans who came to India were seduced and assimilated by India. This love affair with Indians ended decades later when the company firmly established its rule over the people of India and became its undisputed master. The masters grew far away from the people and lived in isolation in parts of the city cantonment they had built, with clubs and parade grounds.

As the days passed, besides their free business opportunities, they were smuggling arms into the country. After fulfilling their real purpose, the spice traders of the John Company finally became the new rulers of India. Soon, they imposed upon the peasantry tax obligations. Even when celebrating their daughter's wedding, the peasants had to pay a fee.

Gradually, the company was able to exploit the differences among the local princes and eventually occupied all of India — except provinces that were occupied by fellow Europeans. Then the British monarch annexed it as British (Occupied) India.

All poor villagers had to work from dawn to dusk as serfs on the fields of landlords. The landlords (zamindars) had been granted the ownership of lands by the British administration in exchange for the payment of fixed land tax.

But how could a British monarch own Indian land? Had they bought it from their Protestant god?

The Fakir and Sanyasi pilgrims were amongst the earliest rebels against British colonial rule in India. Most of them were peasants, who had been dispossessed through wars and the imposition of brutal taxes on their pilgrimage.

All the village poor were subjected to forced labour on the landlord's field; even when young mothers pleaded to their lord, they were denied leave for feeding milk to their newborn babies. They were ordered to show their breasts to put their milk in a container that was sent to the village. To put an end to this crude oppression, female serfs rose in spontaneous revolt.

The Santal community of tribal people rose against this exploitation and oppression; many of them were murdered, flogged, and imprisoned by British exploiters and oppressors.

The Santals were one of the oldest communities to make their home in Bengal. They were largely agrarian people who lived in and depended on forests. After the Britons had occupied India, taxes were levied on the Santals' traditional ways of living. On the other hand, the missionaries of Christianity had taken root in the forests and hills to establish their faith among the natives.

The Santals had traditionally been described as peace-loving, naïve people who had not learnt to lie. These people lived in harmony with their environment. The low population density of indigenous people provided an opportunity for the invasion of the forests by outsiders. Their lands were forcibly taken, and they were lent money at exorbitant rates which they could never repay. They were forced into bonded labour; generation after generation they had to live as serfs, cultivating the zamindar's land just for some food and clothes. Many had no other recourse than to work for Indigo planters or for the frenzy of railway constructions that the British had initiated. And they praised themselves for giving them a job.

Did the Indians hire those Britons? They could hand over the UK to the Japanese, who would rule it better.

The oppression of the Santals and other indigenous communities had festered rebellions over and over again to address their grievances and claim what they had. British guns clashed against bows and arrows and thousands were shot down. Elephants were used to systematically destroy their villages. They viciously suppressed the Santal rebellion.

The Indigo Revolt was renowned in Bengal. Indigo was forcibly cultivated at low prices for the British textile industry. The sapling planters flogged and killed the peasants who dared to protest. Village women were raped at will.

Many other revolts, such as the spontaneous Indigo rebellion and the Tebhaga movement, occurred against British imperialism in various rural districts of Bengal. Peasants, fishermen and artisans transformed into revolutionaries to overthrow the tyranny. The victims had only natural weapons like bows and arrows. The atrocities of British police agents against the suspects included dancing with military boots on their bodies, gang rape and brutal torture.

Oppressed women created their own troops (Nari Bahini) to counter the repression of the authorities. Their weapon of defence was chilli powder.

When the Industrial Revolution began in the West, Britons built railway lines at various strategic positions in vast areas of India. The main concerns were the safe carrying of raw goods for their industries in England, protecting themselves from revolts, and easily transporting weapons in the regions. At that time, a simple gunshot could terrorise thousands of people. This was a key factor that enabled some Protestants to hold millions of Indians hostage to British autocratic rule and allowed them to plunder the country for centuries.

Before the British came, India had a booming export industry with huge trades with countries in the Middle East, Southeast Asia and China. All this had ended by the time they left India. The only consolation was that they left behind a unified structure for administering this vast land.

Not only did undivided India support the Industrial Revolution in England but also British Imperialism by supplying thousands of young men to fight their wars.

India became the jewel of the British crown. In the process they cruelly destroyed indigenous technology, crafts and silk; they saw India as a source of cheap raw materials and labour, and a huge market for goods manufactured in England.

In the end, they destroyed the great benefits of a united India by dividing it on religious lines. Soon after, they watched pleasingly how India and Pakistan (including its eastern part Bangladesh since 1971) were fighting against themselves and not against the British anymore.

Right after the partition, for two long centuries, British crime, tyranny, and cruelty disappeared from the memory of the people of the Indian subcontinent.

## 3.7 Clive, an English spice trader, was a traitor like Mir Jafar (in 1757, Bengal).

If you walk along the path of history, you will see how the Nawab of Bengal, Bihar and Orissa, Siraj-ud-Daulah, was betrayed by his fellow Muslim Mir Jafar, of Arab descent, with whom English Protestant Robert Clive made a secret deal in the darkness of the night. Clive bribed him so that Jafar could work against the Nawab in support of the spice company's soldiers, and in return, Jafar would have been put on the throne of Bengal by Clive.

The Nawab was resentful of the growing influence of the East India Company and the fortressing of the factory. He suspected their expansionist designs of Fort William, which were done without his approval.

Unfortunately, he had enemies in his own family as well. His nomination to the throne led to jealousy and animosity from Ghaseti Begum (the eldest sister of the Nawab's mother).

Siraj made Mohanlal his supreme administrator and Mir Jafar was the head of the armed forces. The elevation of a Hindu to such a prominent position caused some problems in the administration too.

Once the conspiracy of spice traders with Jafar against the Nawab came to light, then Jafar showed great loyalty to the Nawab. He placed his hands on the Quran and swore that he would never betray the Nawab again but would fight hard against the English Christians.

Siraj naïvely believed him because he was a fellow Muslim and pardoned him. But did Jafar take the oath in all honesty? Obviously not; had he done so, the Nawab would not have lost his crown to Clive.

In the critical time of the Plassey battle in 1757, while the Bengal soldiers were on the verge of victory, Mir Jafar tactically pulled out most of the troops from the battlefield under his command. Later, Robert Clive killed the Nawab in cold blood under the guise of Mir Jafar.

These English Christians began their trading company in India by licking the toes of many Nawabs, and this way they paid off their debts.

Mohanlal was a great patriot and the most trusted lieutenant of Siraj who fought valiantly against the English until the end. The word ‘mirjafar’ became synonymous with ‘traitor’ in the history of the Indian subcontinent.

This was how those Englishmen fulfilled their dream of gaining the throne of Bengal. And from thereon, they began to occupy the entire Indian subcontinent under the guise of The East India Company via which they made enormous wealth. A great cultural city, Kolkata (Calcutta), became the company’s headquarters.

In the first quarter of the 16th century, the Mughals entered Delhi on Arabian horsebacks, showing sharp swords with a clear intention of conquering it. And then they fell in love with India and its culture. They ruled India for a long time and made wonderful contributions except for the rule of religion. Muslims contributed a great deal towards the flourishment of Indian melodious music, songs and films, although these are not allowed in Islamic theology. But music is an important part of Hinduism.

Later, Britons entered India in their sailing boats and did not bother to work in servitude at the Mughal emperors’ palaces. Afterwards, as spice traders of John’s company, they created their own soldiers and built fortified buildings surrounded by high and heavy walls where their lords always lived anxiously.

The Mughals built stunning things that everyone could freely see and enjoy. In their impressive sangeet mahal, people were mesmerised by the melodious voices of singers and dancers. The emperors were relaxed, playing chess, and wandering freely in nature. They paid no real attention to what the English merchants were clandestinely doing in India.

Alexander the Great conquered the whole civilised world with his strength, and courage, and led the battles himself that made him the Great. His intention was quite clear.

At the beginning of the 13th century, a Muslim warrior of Turkic origin Muhammad Bakhtiyar Khalji attacked the kingdom of Bengal and conquered it without resistance. He was leading only 17 horsemen with him; and that was enough for King Lakshman Sen. On hearing about the horse race, the king simply left his palace, without even trying to know who the enemy was. That was the end of the last independent ruler of Bengal. Thereafter, Khalji’s sharp swords were responsible for the spread of Islam in Bengal.

## 3.8 Curzon, an English Protestant, divided Bengal for Muslims and Hindus in 1905 to deceive people.

Khudiram Bose, a seven to eight-year-old boy, devoted himself to thinking, "India is our country. When I grow up, I must drive the British out of India."

Once, the young boy Khudiram was following a conversation about diseases in a temple when someone asked him, "What disease has struck you?" He replied, "What can be a worse disease than slavery?"

When and how could a child's brain be confronted with such questions?

In 1905, Curzon devised a new plan to divide Bengal into East and West Bengal in the name of religious majority. Mawlana Azad, a Muslim and learned revolutionary leader, was against the British's nasty policies for India. Without distinction of any religion, they opposed the partition of Bengal in one voice.

It was at this time that Khudiram, at the age of 16, initiated a revolution. In February 1906, during a grand exhibition at Medinipur, he defied the British police by distributing handbills and bravely exposed its hidden motives.

While he was just 18, he threw his first bomb against the autocratic regimes on April 30, 1908. On August 11, he was hanged by the British. What surprised everyone was that while he was being hanged, he was still cheerful and smiling. He remains immortal in the history of India.

To spread communal violence, British Christian agents slaughtered pigs in mosques and slaughtered cows in temples, where India's diverse spiritual people had been living in natural harmony long before the birth of Christianity.

## 3.9 The massacre of a British General at the Sikh annual festival in Amritsar, Punjab, in 1919, alarmed the world.

On April 13, 1919, the day of the Sikh Baisakhi, about 13,000 people including men, women and children, from nearby villages had come to Amritsar to attend the city's annual religious and cultural festival at Jallianwala Bagh.

More than a million Indians fought for Britain in the First World War alone, around 60,000 of them were killed. Immediately after the war, pressure for India's independence mounted. Previously, the English had promised this on several occasions. But never did they keep their promises. After the movement of Indian nationalists during the war, Britons once again promised, "After this war, India will be free, as we are now in a war, so you Indians, please fight our war first."

After the end of the First World War, they yet again overlooked the promises they had made; instead of talking about Indian independence, the British government introduced new conscriptions to force Indians to serve the British Army for their potential war elsewhere. Besides, they imposed a heavy war tax on Indian people. In reaction to this, a few days prior, there were nonviolent protests in the city; and just a few days later, the traditional Sikh festival was being held at Jallianwala Bagh on April 13.

On hearing about the gathering, the British commander Brigadier General Dyer entered the Bagh (Garden) with 90 troops. The garden was walled on all sides with only a few entrances. They locked the exit and started shooting indiscriminately at those who were enjoying their traditional celebrations.

All of a sudden, the men, women and children at the festival were stunned. They screamed and began running like flocks of sheep to escape the carnage, but they were trapped. They ran towards the other entrance, but Dyer's guns continued to rain bullets on them. Some jumped into a deep well but drowned. The commander and his soldiers continued to fire and relished the reality that Indians, who were trapped between bullets and closed entrances, were falling like ninepins. He only stopped when they ran out of ammunition.

By then, the actual death toll had reached close to 1,000; and there were over 1,400 wounded. The General left the place with his troops, looking very proudly at the dead and wounded who lay screaming on the ground.

A terrorist like this man in the British Army did not receive any punishment for such a barbaric act. After this cold-blooded murder when he returned to Britain, he was widely welcomed as their hero; even the House of Lords honoured him for the cruelty he committed on behalf of the British Crown.

This attitude of the British monarchy clearly defined what state-sponsored terrorism really was.

Clothed in civilised uniform in which Commander Dyer felt very proud, he killed innocent people in a way that marked the ugliness of British colonial rule.

Plundering fortunes from one country to distribute it in their own land was a common policy of the British Monarchy. One such thing is still glittering in the queen's ornaments, the fabled diamond, the Kohinoor of India — which was stolen by the British spice merchants of the East India Company. Yet they deny that they were thieves but instead were masters.

With their guns, they terrorised and murdered many innocent civilians every time they took over their land and resources.

What Officer Dyer wanted to convey via his barbaric act was that if Indians ever wanted India's independence again, they would get such lessons from British Christians, so Indians would have to hold their tongues and let the occupiers first steal India's wealth. The Britons felt proud of killing unarmed people in confinement, and their House of Lords, too, showed the same characteristic as Dyer.

## 3.10 The 21st century emerges with a new form of terrorism, but nobody knows its definition.

Very recently, western gangs have occupied oil-rich Iraq at the beginning of this new millennium; instead of breastfeeding for their good health, they are sucking Saddam's oil for their industries' health but still saying that they have not gone there for oil.

Blair, led by Bush, premeditatedly lied about Saddam and went against the opinion of the whole world to invade Iraq.

Never before had I seen so many public demonstrations everywhere in the globe against going to war for oil. That tells me that ordinary people from all over the planet understand the fact, and they are compassionate and kind-hearted. Even in London, there were several huge public demonstrations against the government. To be honest, I could not believe those Britons had hearts, too.

Nevertheless, Blair and Bush defied not only the people but also the United Nations; yet, they pompously say they are the promoters of democracy and human rights. Can anyone be a more brutal dictator and extremist than them?

At the UN, France led the way against the falsification of the UK and the US to invade Iraq. Belgium was also against the pretext of this aggression; but being a small country, it finally had to join in because when the conflict was outside of the West their master's unjust policy was to bring them all on board by any means.

Iraq's deputy prime minister and Saddam's long-time close friend Tariq Aziz (a Christian) went to the Vatican to meet the Pope. Aziz was a great critic of Bush. He requested the Pope to press for peace in the Middle East and to prevent Bush from going to war for oil in Iraq.

The Catholic Pope expressed his resentment against the Anglo-American intentions. But soon after Aziz's visit, Blair (a Protestant) went to the Vatican with his Catholic wife to oil the Pope (head of the Catholic Church). He was likely able to persuade the Pope to get Iraqi oil to survive the economic growth of the West.

Blair always said that Saddam was a liar; Blair lied hypocritically in every breath; the British Parliament led by Tony Blair proudly passed a blatantly false resolution that Saddam possessed weapons of mass destruction and that those weapons were pointing to London and Washington to obliterate them at any time. The BBC had been persistently propagating these false accusations against Saddam Hussein.

The West politically do not call themselves Christians, but aggressively they have always been so. They themselves have weapons of mass destruction, but if somebody else develops such weapons, they are scared. They like to show off their muscles to those who do not have muscle, and this is their pride.

They were the ones who used atomic weapons, whereas they bogusly accused someone who had no such weapons.

At the UN, before the invasion, Blair and Bush presented fake evidence against Saddam that he possessed weapons of mass destruction. And their agent Richard Butler, who acted as the United Nations' chief weapons inspector, echoed with the duo. However, the UN did not agree. Still, the pair went against the world's opinion and occupied Iraq. Surprisingly, they did not find any such weapons in Saddam's Iraq.

What surprised the world the most is that the UN, which presumably represents the world, did nothing against Blair and Bush — the two utmost war criminals in the world — but instead endorsed the Anglo-American invasion of Iraq. Isn't the UN merely a puppet organisation of the West?

Bush annexed Iraq as a new state of the USA and immediately appointed his man as governor in Baghdad.

The US administration in occupied Iraq has turned the whole country into a grave of disaster. Their governor lives in a heavily fortified area of Baghdad. Their pocket media that cannot go freely to any other areas of Baghdad is broadcasting fabricated news about Iraq to fool the people. And the naïve people of the world are swallowing the news of the invaders.

The West has deliberately killed some independent journalists of the world media in Iraq.

Modern gangsters of Christianity have stolen valuables from museums in Baghdad and elsewhere in Iraq; much evidence of one of the oldest civilisations in the world has been lost. They have destroyed the Iraqis' beautiful country and infrastructure and killed hundreds of thousands of civilians after the invasion.

They expected that the people of Iraq would welcome them with a bunch of roses, but the western occupiers now live in the hell that they have created to seize Iraqi oil and soil, something that was not possible for them when Saddam was in power. However, now they are constantly extracting free oil from Iraq.

The mighy duo, Bush-Blair, did not dare to celebrate victory with the Iraqis, nor did they ever dare to go to Iraq to talk to the people of Iraq.

The rest of Iraq is virtually no-man's-land. Chaos and anarchy — misery pervades every corner of the country. Large numbers of people are fleeing and becoming refugees elsewhere; those who are there are mostly living in the horrors of hell.

The US governor luckily survived a heavy Iraqi attack in his greatest security position. He had survived similar attacks before. But a few days after this, he fled Iraq. Obviously, in a civilised style.

Now under a puppet government in Iraq, the US occupation continues behind the door. After Saddam, the country is in a state of extreme turmoil. But the Americans are full of praise, saying they have freed the Iraqis from the hands of the dictator.

Saddam was a dictator of his own country and his people; Bush on the other hand, was not only a dictator of his own country in the shadow of democracy but also a dictator of the world during his rule.

Why do they not learn to speak the truth? Maybe their god likes them because they are the mightiest. But will their own people like them if they are misinformed?

They are the masters of institutional injustice, torture, and brutal killings. They run secret terrorist camps to grab other people's wealth, and when those terrorists go against them, they shout for war on terror.

Bush and Blair, the two most powerful Christians, are the greatest child killers in the history of humankind, whereas they clamour for human rights. They run underground torture camps to which no human rights organisation has any access.

Those international 'rights organisations' never raise such issues seriously, in which the West is involved.

During the 1980s, when there was an eight-year-long war between Iran and Iraq, the USA was selling weapons to Iraq as a great friend of Saddam and a foe of Iran. In 1986, it came to light that despite the US arms embargo on Iran, it was secretly and illegally selling weapons to Iran at the same time.

This top-secret underground arms trafficking is known as the Iran-gate Scandal. This smuggling by the US government was taking place via Israel; so that the world could never identify who the smugglers were. Ronald Reagan was president, and George Bush was his vice president; they were routinely telling their people that Iran was a terrorist country, so America imposed an arms embargo against the Iranians in the interest of the earth.

But fortunately, what the world got to know through the Iran-gate Scandal was that the president of the most powerful country was cheating the people of the world. What he and his vice president were telling their own people during the day about Iran, and what they were doing at night was a symbol of their great civilised character.

They felt no shame but again rewrote the history of their lives the way they liked. This is their way of life and pride. They once again go to church and ask people to beware of the devils, and the Fathers of the church bless them as the greatest protectors of god.

Blair has proved himself to be the biggest terrorist in this world so far. He has broken the record of Bin Laden by a huge margin, who had been holding the title since 2001.

Bush and Blair took the whole world with them against Osama Bin Laden, who operated his machine gun against the whole world from a cave in Afghanistan. When some western countries do something together, they always say that the whole world is with them.

The western military superpowers tried hard to bring India along with them as part of the attacking forces against Afghanistan but failed. India also did not allow western allies to use its territory to attack Afghanistan. So, they badly needed Pakistan's strategic land route for their forces in Afghanistan. Pakistan has fallen into the trap of Bush and Blair and is now paying a heavy price.

Historical evidence exists that British Christians often chose Muslims to punish Muslims.

Without president Pervez Musharraf's direct involvement with Bush and Blair, the West could not have launched a terrorist attack in Afghanistan so easily, destroying the entire country and then occupying it.

Pakistan has been a victim of terrorism by its own people, by the Taliban and by the US. When the US-led aggressors have settled comfortably in Afghanistan, they blame Pakistan for not doing enough to fight the terrorists.

The West has gone to Afghanistan to root out terrorism from the world; the result, however, is that terrorists are now everywhere around the globe. So, the United States is now childishly accusing Pakistan for it.

On the morning hours of September 11, 2001, Bin Laden astonishes the whole world by occupying the sky of the USA — hijacking some of their big aeroplanes filled with fuel; the first plane attacks one of the world's tallest twin towers, which begins to crumble to pieces altogether; this seems to wake up Americans to the fact that Bin Laden is there, and that they can see him directly, live.

Just minutes later, the second plane hits the second twin that is collapsing likewise, leaving more than 3,000 people dead. And the third plane hits the Pentagon, the military headquarters of the world's most powerful country, destroying a large part of it.

Bush flees the White House and says it is the work of Bin Laden. Blair repeats this claim at once. Their massive media immediately echoes with them and says that Saudi billionaire Osama Bin Laden has carried out the biggest terrorist attack in America. Similarly, the world media is repeating the same.

Bush and Blair assured the world that they would bring Bin Laden to justice and demanded that Afghanistan hand over Bin Laden to them.

The Afghan government asked them to provide proof that he has indeed carried out such a horrible terrorist attack. But they could not provide any evidence, so the poor Afghans refused to concede to the demand of the world's élite power.

Bush and Blair declare that they will forcefully bring Bin Laden out of Afghanistan and put him on trial. And then they start bombarding Afghanistan from north to south and from west to east; in the process, house after house and mountain after mountain are demolished just for a man.

Once they spotted Bin Laden in a cave in the Tora Bora Mountains, as they claimed; BBC correspondents reported that Bin Laden is in the cave and is surrounded by US-led Allied forces; yes, yes, he is hiding there; it is only a matter of hours now before they catch him.

Within a few hours, the media has disappeared from the cave and chased Osama's sweat.

He once again appears on the world media stage.

Each time he appears on the media, the West says that they will verify if it is the voice of Bin Laden. But never did they report the result of their verification.

If they thought that they had supernatural powers and knew that Osama had masterminded such an unimaginably bloody attack from a cave in Afghanistan, why did they let him succeed in doing so?

What were the CIA officers doing? For such a daring operation that involved heavy training of the pilots in the United States and many other things, and then getting such work done from Afghanistan was not a simple task. At least four of their (US) big aeroplanes were hijacked from their different airports around the same time. The planes departed from one end of the USA to its other end — flying full of fuel and passengers — targeting the objects precisely — accelerating the speed and finally — making the whole operation a success, was not the work of a day.

Could any intelligent agency of the West ever have imagined that such an attack could take place in any other country? But it happened in the heart of mighty America. It was their people, their planes, their airports, and in their powerful country where it happened. Why didn't Bush bomb their CIA headquarters, instead of continually killing Afghans who had nothing to do with it?

How can the governments of other civilised countries of the world tolerate this? How have they been continually witnessing such heinous crimes over the years? How can the UN endorse such unforgivable brutalities?

However, from time to time, Osama shows himself on the world screen as a ghost of the western world; they can no longer say from which Afghan cave he is running the world media.

But they resume their bombing raids in Afghanistan at will, which has been going on month after month and year after year. Wherever and whenever they see people gathering, wedding ceremonies, religious and cultural celebrations, they bombard, killing thousands of people every month, as they are so afraid of the image of Laden.

Just for a man, they have murdered countless men, women and children, totally destroying the country.

This is not terrorism at all. Because white Christians cannot be terrorists; they are the sons of god. They do not kill humans; they only kill terrorists who are against their god. This is why they keep no records of how many people they murder each day.

By now, the whole world knows that the definition of a terrorist is narrow and confined to only those instances where a white Christian is attacked by a Muslim, then by the western definition — Muslims are terrorists. In contrast, when a Muslim is attacked by a Christian, Christians are called the great peacemakers on earth. The word 'terrorist' therefore has no other objective meaning except as a political word.

What the people of the world have witnessed is that Muslim terrorists are individuals or organisations. Christian terrorists, however, are not individuals; their government is doing such atrocious things.

They started the so-called war on terrorism in October 2001 — to date, they are still incapable of bringing the perpetrator of the horrendous criminal attacks on the Twin Towers and the Pentagon to justice. But they are still killing Afghans indiscriminately.

Meanwhile, after occupying Afghanistan in the name of Bin Laden, they invaded Iraq. And in the same style and rhythm — they have been killing Iraqis for years.

Bin Laden took only a couple of hours to accomplish his biggest terrorist mission in the US. Since then, the real world has been eagerly waiting to see who Osama Bin Laden actually is. A lot of people have nightmares about him. Only Bush knows that Laden carried out the attack because he had a great business relationship with him, but why can he not still present him to the world as promised? Instead, he is killing innocent people like the rat population of Afghanistan.

Bin Laden's September 11 terror attacks are not that terrible compared to the number of people killed in Britain by Gerry Adams's terror attacks.

The IRA of Sinn Fein in Ireland has been a well-known terrorist organisation to the British for many years. The head of the IRA, Gerry Adams, a Catholic, carried out many terrorist attacks in Britain; the British army tried to kill him many times. But after the terrorist attacks in New York and the Pentagon, he was not referred to as terrorist anymore. For the sake of Christianity, the British government may have hastily compromised with their famous terrorist Gerry Adams in the face of a heavyweight terrorist like Bin Laden, a Muslim. Interestingly, Blair never bombarded Northern Ireland to get Gerry Adams, nor did Bush come to help him eliminate terrorism from the world.

Since the deadly September 11 attacks, the West had said Saudi billionaire Osama Bin Laden did this. Days later, they dropped the phrase 'Saudi billionaire' from the news.

The United States operates a top-secret torture centre in Guantanamo; those who have been detained and tortured there have not been charged with any crime and have not been convicted. Many Afghans were taken and tortured there only to learn about Bin Laden's whereabouts. The world is well aware of the long business relationship that George Bush had with Osama. Why did George destroy all traces of that friendship with Osama, and why did he torture Afghans in that vicious torture camp?

Just after attacking Iraq, they said that Saddam fled to another country to save his life, but a patriotic Saddam was still fighting against the mighty aggressors. So when he was captured, they put him in a secret place to humiliate his patriotism;

months later, in their holy month of December, they presented him to the media as a Christmas present, pretending that he had been in a deep hole for several months. This is one of the premeditated sins of Christianity, which the real world will always remember, and their god, too, if he is not the personal god of white Christians.

The white colonial groups used Osama as a pretext to invade Afghanistan, a geo-strategically important country, to test and train them with the newly developed dangerous war machinery and then to attack oil-rich Iraq. As another excuse, they wanted to be doubly sure that Saddam did not possess any weapons that could pose a threat to them, so they used the UN's chief weapons inspector (an Australian Christian), who had made a series of inspections in Iraq over the years.

They imposed a no-fly zone to weaken the country first and made plenty of unusual visits to Iraq, which also happened in Bill Clinton's era, with inspectors themselves finding no such weapon of mass destruction. In addition, the inspectors of the team praised the Iraqis for their excellent hospitality. But once again, another proposal was made by the most powerful western leaders of the United Nations that they should be allowed to visit Saddam's Presidential Palace. He even allowed this; they searched every nook and corner of the palace more than once, but the outcome was never different.

It was only when they were absolutely certain that Saddam Hussein was not a threat to them that the most powerful democracies quickly occupied Iraq. Soon after, at first, they plundered all the invaluable things of a great ancient civilisation.

Are they not terrorists in the shadow of democracy?

The US alone could have destroyed Iraq, but it could not have occupied it. Compared to the Iraqis, they were mentally very weak, and their morale was also weak because their reasons for the invasion were based on mere lies. But their weapons of mass destruction made their people warmongers.

They dropped atomic bombs on Hiroshima and Nagasaki when Japan had already started surrendering; the US did this horrendous act to scare other people around the world, not them. Secondly, they used Japanese soil to test their weapons of mass destruction and to demonstrate the monstrous power of Christians, which could kill millions of innocent people with just one nuclear drop.

## 3.11 Modern humans are very destructive and inhumane.

The West or the First World has recently banned imports of natural or Third World products where children under the age of 18 are working, calling it 'child labour'.

The US military recently used 'child soldiers' to capture Iraq. The British recruited 'child soldiers' in India, Australia, and other colonies; they committed this inhumane act by force.

The Australian government has been forcibly stealing Aboriginal children from their homes for centuries. Thousands of children have been placed into strictly religious institutions, where, as orphans, they would be sexually and physically abused. This hidden official act still exists, and it has caused widespread anger. Many other stolen indigenous generations were adopted into white families. Many never realised the fact; some, somehow, nevertheless questioned themselves and made a remarkable journey to find their biological families. That revealed the traumatic experiences of them being taken away from their homes by the official Australian secret policy; where the British monarch still reigns today.

The British Crown has done nothing for the suffering of the people to redress British trafficking of Africans in the Caribbean and elsewhere, and the enslavement that took place during the period of the present Queen Elizabeth II and her predecessors.

The West has been enjoying extremely high profits from their industrial products for centuries; now some industrial sectors in the natural world are becoming more price competitive than westerners. This may be a new headache for them to go against the children of the Third World pretending to sympathise with them.

A human under the age of 18 is, indeed, a child by legal definition, but children in the natural world are generally seen to be much more active in practical work environments than in the western world. However, irrespective of the western or eastern world, if a child is capable and willingly does a certain thing, what is wrong there? I feel learning by experience is a very good, interesting, and creative thing.

What I cannot digest, however, is how can a little baby be baptised as a Christian?

If white people do not know something, they pompously say — if we don't know it, then no one knows. Do they believe they were born before the Indigenous people?

Individual persons of any race can somehow be racist, but how can a civilised government make racial segregation laws to treat black people as wild animals? Is it the right of white people to hate others by enacting such laws? Is this the human right they believe in? To Anglo-Americans, all colours, except white, are coloured.

While a well-clothed Gandhi sat in the first-class compartment of a train in South Africa, he was asked, "How dare you come to this compartment!"

"Well, I bought a first-class ticket, sir."

"It is not for coloured people!" He was then thrown out of the train by the white officer.

Human beings are humane and inhumane, which has nothing to do with their civilisation or religion, but with their mindset towards society.

No other creatures fight against one another, except humans, with anything other than what their god has given them. In this regard, all humans are maybe wiser than donkeys. Have you ever realised that elephants are very humane?

The people of India were living in natural and spiritual peace. But they were blown away by British imperialism and adopted the myopia of Eurocentric materialism and broke away from their 5,000-year-old heritage.

When Indians began to manufacture weapons, the modern British were asking, "why does India make arms, when it cannot feed its people." Now they have established a special relationship with it. India is now selling arms to become rich.

Instead of learning from spiritual India, Britons prolonged their occupation of the Indian subcontinent by taking advantage of the non-violent movement. Netaji Subhas Chandra Bose understood this very clearly. This was the only difference between him and Mahatma Gandhi in the long struggle of our ancestors to drive the British occupiers out of India.

The imperialists jailed both of them many times in their own land because people of all colours in India loved them and came to listen to them in huge numbers.

In South Africa, the white regime imprisoned Gandhi several times only because of his nonviolent movement against apartheid and because they could not answer his questions. If he had reacted violently, what would they have done then?

After returning to India, he was weaving his own clothes and wore a simple piece of traditional cloth.

During the Quit India movement, a full-fledged rich-white prime minister commented, "It is alarming and nauseating to see Mr. Gandhi, now posing as a fakir of a type well known in the east, striding half-naked up the steps of the Vice Regal Palace."

If pacifists keep their doors open while sleeping at night believing that everyone on earth is like them, then evil humans, not beasts, will enter the houses of pacifists and loot valuables. If they resist, the perpetrators will preach, "These people are not pacifists; they are violent, too." The oppressors always think that they have the right to rule peaceful people at will, and the oppressed have no right to oppose them. Robbers may kill pacifists who will protest and occupy their houses forever. Eventually, the true history of those ancient houses may no longer exist.

Gandhi invented a unique humane means against apartheid, racial segregation, inhumanity, and atrocities of British imperialists in South Africa and India. They responded with arms against his humane approach. Brutality by weapons can enslave people for a certain period but not win their hearts even for a moment.

Mahatma Gandhi taught the imperialists quite a different lesson. He was a unique icon of peace in the modern world. Gandhiji's teachings remain immortal in inspiring pacifists across the world, even many British admire his great heart.

## 3.12 Are we Muslims by faith, by birth, by name, or by proselytising?

From Pakistan to Arab countries, a Muslim connection is visible, but how did Bengal become so Islam-oriented? No country in the vicinity is an Islamic nation-state.

The face of a person does not tell his or her religion but rather one's native origin. Everywhere in the world, people bear their family names; but in Bengal, most Muslims do not carry their family names. Why is this so? Perhaps we do not know our ancestors' history, or perhaps we want to intentionally hide our roots. Even in the same family, one person's full name is completely different from another's. A stranger cannot be sure if they belong to the same family.

Many Hindus have been converted into Muslims in our country, but where are they living in our society?

The preachers who proselytise through coercive means cannot be believers of the creator. They completely root out the original name and familial identity of a transformed person to show that the person has always been a believer of their religion. Proselytising by bullying is an act of deceiving people.

It is not shameful if you convert to another religion of your own free will; in fact, it enlightens your confidence. But if you knowingly deny your true origin and completely destroy the roots of your family, that means your faith is doubtful. Can you hide your blood identity?

The first name of most Bengali Muslim children is usually a Bengali name at birth; but during the registration for Secondary School Certificate (SSC) examinations, many of them are given the so-called 'good name' i.e., mainly an Arab name, excluding their birth name. However, to their family and friends, they are always known by their birth names. As there is no official birth registration system, the birth dates of a considerable number of students at this time are written based on assumptions. Sometimes schools do it on behalf of their students. This is the reference record of their names and births. There are so many people who never go to school, and many students drop out of school before registering for these exams.

My first or birth name was 'Shaupaun' (স্বপন). Since I was born in a Muslim family, my birth name vanished and was replaced by Kawsar without a family name. My age was wrong. After coming abroad, I realised the importance of a family name. And I wanted my Bengali birth name and correct date of birth in the official documents of my native and immigrant countries. For this, I had to go through all the annoying and lengthy legal processes.

In Libya (1977), an Arab was talking to us (some Bangladeshis) and asked, "What do you say in your language when you meet someone?"

We all replied, "We say assalamu alaikum."

"Is Arabic your language?" he questioned curiously.

"How can you think like that!" we reacted. "Our language isn't Arabic; it's Bengali."

"Oh, really! So why do you say assalamu alaikum? That's what our Arabic speakers say."

"You actually don't know anything brother, as you're Muslim, we're Muslim too. You and we are the same people; therefore, when we meet someone, we say assalamu alaikum."

"It's good that your people have embraced our religion"; he responded, "in this case, obviously our religion is the same. But you're not Arabs, you can't speak Arabic, and you don't look like us too. That is why I wanted to know: as in the morning, we say sabah al-khair and sabah al-noor; don't you say something like that in your mother tongue?"

"Yes, of course, Hindus say — namaskar."

"What you're saying sounds strange! Here, we Muslims, Christians and Jews are all Arabs. Arabic is our mother tongue. When we speak Arabic, it's very natural to say assalamu alaikum, but it doesn't mean that everybody here is Muslim. People's religion and ethnic identity aren't the same thing. When a person speaks a language, they speak to their cultural rhythm. But your Bengali language seems very interesting. You Muslims say assalamu alaikum, and Hindus say namaskar:

what do Christians and people belonging to other religions say? Does that mean when you go anywhere and before you say namaskar or assalamu alaikum, you first ask what their religion is?"

Our pundit-like words have already been exhausted.

If your educated bigoted mind is filled with other people's opinions without contemplation, then being illiterate is not really a bad thing.

One day a Bangladeshi saw a page of Arabic writing lying on the street; he immediately went there and kissed the page as though he was greatly honoured.

One of our Libyan colleagues inquisitively asked him, "Why did you kiss it?"

"How can your people throw this page of the holy Quran on the street!" he questioned in dismay.

The Libyan read it at once; then he let it fall to the ground and rubbed the page under his shoes and rolled with laughter.

The questioner with startled eyes looked at him for a long time and said, "If you were a true Muslim, you couldn't do this."

"If you had known how to read Arabic," says the Libyan, eyes gleaming, "then you wouldn't have kissed this page as the page of the holy Quran; it's an article about an Egyptian film actress. Please try to recognise your own ignorance first before questioning the religious beliefs of others."

When I recall my vivid reminiscences of Libya, this scene often comes to my mind. But this memory is quite different. Never before have I had this experience.

If these two incidents had not happened in an Islamic country and in front of the native Muslims, I would probably have judged them differently.

## 3.13 Communalism as an attitude of hatred in the name of religion exists in our Bengali language as well.

Why do Bengali Muslims say *pani* instead of *jaul*? Many Bangladeshi Muslims think that if you say *jaul*, you are a Hindu. So, when an Englishman says water for water, does it mean he is a Christian? The word 'Mr' is used before the name of an Englishman, and they use it for a Muslim man too. We do not mind then, but we have an objection to the word 'Sri'. Arabs have no problem when they are addressed by Sri, but why cannot we accept it? Maybe the word Sri reminds us of the real origin, which hurts us. So why is Bengali our mother tongue?

During the Pakistan period, Muslims used to say 'Khoda Hafez', and now they have converted it into 'Allah Hafez'. If you think of them as Pakistani Muslims, that is probably why they have dropped half the phrase after their separation from Pakistan. But what about the other half? The words *saheb* and *memsaheb* mean white Europeans. Why do we like to expose ourselves to a fake cultural identity?

If a woman says bonjour, it simply indicates that she speaks French; it does not show her religion; likewise, if a man says good night, it does not mean that he is a Christian. But while you speak English and say assalamu alaikum, you publicise that you are a Muslim.

An Arab Muslim does not hesitate to say namasté while speaking in Hindi. When an Indian Bengali speaks in Hindi, he no longer uses the word *jaul* but *pani*. Bangladeshi Muslims, however, are filled with shyness when it comes to the word *jaul*. Interestingly, the word *jaul* is a Bengali word; *pani* is a Hindi word.

Instead of using some Arabic words in Bengali to identify yourselves as Muslims of Arab descent, why don't you speak Arabic?

Such is the nature of wicked people that they go against those from whom they got help to hide the fact that they once got help from them or the relationship they once had with them. We now very gladly kiss the English and American Christians who were against our freedom. But all the time we hate Hindus from whom our ancestors were born.

Bangladesh, once a vivid cultural country, has now become a state of fanaticism. We are so desperate to get a false cultural identity that after 1971 we have come down from a Muslim sky.

You may succeed in hiding yourself in your country to pretend that you are from somewhere else rather than your surroundings. But once you go into the arena of the world, cultural people will easily find your roots just by looking at your face.

India is not only our neighbouring country but also the land of our great ancestors. Bangladesh is surrounded by Hindu India; moreover, from generation to generation, we have long cultural and familial ties with ancient Hindustan. Never will you be able to escape your geographical and cultural boundaries through lies.

## 3.14 The trio of Bengal — Girish, Rokeya and Dukhu.

Girish Chandra Sen (1835-1910) became a great sensation all over India by presenting the first Bengali version of the Quran. But his place in our Muslim society is very small. He was a Bengali scholar who was born in Narayanganj in Dhaka district and died in Calcutta, the capital of Bengal. Many Muslims were keen to convert Sen into a Muslim but did not succeed.

If they could have given him at least one Muslim name, he would have been highly respected by Bengali Muslims. This was the first time they were able to read and understand their sacred book in Bengali, which had been written in Arabic many centuries ago.

We superstitious Muslims prefer to rely on those Muslims who do not understand the language of the Quran but can only recite it. We hate Girish Chandra Sen because he is not a Muslim, but he knows the language of the Quran. We like dogmatists because they are Muslims; but who knows whether they were Hindus and converted to Islam out of fear or greed?

After the attacks of Muslims and Christians in Hindustan and the colonial oppression of peasants, most scheduled caste Hindus were massively converted to other religions. Once upon a time, they loved Bhagavan. Now they are very fond of Allah, who allows them to do things they could not have done before. What can you expect from these Muslims? They have simply changed their traditional belief and become loudspeakers of Islam. After each prayer and ritual, they allocate bonus points to the worshippers.

It was forbidden to study anything other than Arabic in the Muslim community. Due to this ill-motivated attitude, Muslims were far behind in the field of general education in India.

Begum Rokeya (1880-1932) was born into an orthodox Muslim family in Rangpur, Bengal, Colonial India. The system of solitude (Pardha) was maintained as the religious duty of Muslim women.

She and her sisters received only religious education at home, which was the tradition of reading Arabic. Their father was opposed to educating his daughters.

Rokeya's elder brother secretly taught her Bengali and English at home as clerics threatened her for violating Islamic law. And her entire family was cut off from the Muslim community. How can Muslim clerics live in countries around the world that are not Islamic?

When she got married at the age of sixteen, her Urdu-speaking Muslim husband understood her position against Islamic doctrine about women. He then encouraged her to continue in Bengali, so that she could express her views through her writings. Living in Bihar, Rokeya got all the support she needed from her Bihari husband to cure the ills of her society.

Through her writings, she criticised the oppressive social norms imposed on women in the name of religion, claiming that the glory of divinity could best be demonstrated by women who fulfilled their potential as human beings.

She died in Calcutta in 1932. Throughout her life, she proved herself to be a humanist rather than a Muslim. She used to say, "We are not only Hindus, Muslims, Parsis, Sikhs … or Bengalis, Biharis, Marwaris, Punjabis … we are Indians first and then the rest."

When Rokeya was honoured by other communities, those who insulted and issued fatwas against her praised her as if she were their dearest heroine. They felt no shame for what they did against her, and what they were doing with her statue thereafter.

Dukhu Mia, the birth name of Kazi Nazrul Islam, strongly opposed superstitions and religious intolerance. Muslim dogmatic mullahs denounced him as kafir (atheist) and tried to harm him in various ways but could not succeed as he was not a superstitious man. He boldly went against those mullahs and became a rebel poet (bidrohi kaubi).

Mia was born in 1899 in a hardship-ridden Muslim family in a village called Churulia in undivided Bengal, India. At the age of about ten, he lost his father who was the caretaker of a local mosque. From a very young age, Dukhu had to go through a lot of hardships; he took his father's place as the caretaker of the mosque and then did all sorts of things not only for his own livelihood but also for the rest of his family.

Later, while working with a rural theatrical group, he came to know about poetry, drama and literature, which led him to settle down in Calcutta (Kolkata), which was then the cultural capital city of India.

Although Muslim by birth, he was a man of love, freedom, humanity and revolution. He was a great critic of religious dogma and intolerance. Mia's powerful writings hit hard against social ills. He also stood firm against British autocratic rule and injustice in India. Hence, he was also well-known as the rebel poet.

He fell in love with Hindu Pramila Devi and got married to her. This got him into abundant trouble with the rest of his family, and of course, it was a great moment for Islamic scholars to vehemently condemn him. If he had given Pramila a Islamic name, he would have been saved from the humiliation inflicted on him by Muslims.

However, Dukhu completely ignored his fellow Muslim community. He became more revolutionary by speaking against bigotry in his clear voice. His poems articulated the aspirations of the downtrodden naïve people of the society and their emancipation.

His nationalist activism and patriotic songs for Indian independence led the colonial British Christians to jail him several times. Many of his publications were banned. He was not allowed to walk in his own land, talk to his people, or express himself in songs. But Dukhu was such an inspirational man that even while in prison, he assailed the British imperialists and spoke of revolution through his poetic works.

In 1942, at the age of 43, he lost his voice and memory forever. In May 1972, he came to Dacca (Dhaka) at the invitation of the Mujib government of the newly independent Bangladesh and with the consent of the Indira government. He died there in August 1976. In January 1976, he was given citizenship of Bangladesh by the military regime and by that time he did not understand what it meant.

The trio — Girish, Rokeya and Dukhu — though they are all ethnically Bengalis, are all pure Indians first.

Why has Rokeya suddenly become so dear in Bangladesh? How can Muslims erect her statue and polish it so nicely? Is there a smell of Islam in her statue just because she was born in Rangpur?

Sen was born in Narayanganj, why is he not even known to many Muslim gurus? If they were true believers in Allah, and if Girish Chandra Sen were born in Israel, they would have loved Girish as much as Rokeya. Above all, the holy book of the Bengali Muslims was in Arabic, which we do not understand; therefore, Girish has given us a wonderful gift — *the Bengali Quran*.

Why have Muslims now taken Dukhu on their heads, whom they threw at their feet calling him an infidel? The only plausible answer to this could be that he was born into a Muslim family. Hence, the Imams may be trying to pit him against Rabindranath. But it could only be for bad intentions. Nazrul expressed strong anger against the Islamic fatwas and the mullahs. On the other hand, he had immense devotion to Rabindranath and his country India. Rabindranath loved him so much, and they were both very good friends because they were both Indian Bengalis.

Bangladesh is not for Muslims, but for Bengalis created by the people of Bengal. Pakistan (1947) was created for Muslims by a few Indian Muslim leaders who did not ask the people of Bengal to decide whether to go with Pakistan or not. As a result, 24 years later, the ordinary Bengalis totally rejected the Islamic gurus' theory of creating Pakistan, and were born anew as a secular Bangladesh (1971).

When Pakistan was created for Muslims, Dukhu Mia did not join us, nor did we dare bring him to our Muslim Bengal; because then our religious mullahs knew very well that he was fiercely against them. Never did he support the separation of humans based on their religious bloodlines.

After Bangladesh emerged as a secular state, Dukhu Nazrul's family brought him to visit Bangladesh at the invitation of the Mujib government because he was a great motivating spirit for the Bengali nation. Since he could no longer speak, the Islamists who had once declared him an unbeliever took it as an opportunity to play a tricky religious game.

Nazrul was neither born in Bangladesh nor East Bengal of Pakistan; he was born in Bengal (West) in India and lived there. Hence, he had nothing to do with our present-day Bangladesh. He was a pure Indian. But now who are those who call him our national hero?

Rokeya went against Islamic law and showed women living in a safe human cave — the way out of the darkness to observe the beauty of the sun.

Dukhu Nazrul went further away; he completely rejected the idea of theological Islam and revolted to overcome the barriers of religion. He lashed out at self-proclaimed religious leaders or mullahs for keeping women in seclusion where their women were dying due to lack of light and fresh air.

Nazrul lived in the country where he was born and grew up. India is a unique country, where all religious and non-religious people are accepted; even many primitive religious communities are living there in peace, love, and harmony.

Dukhu was a very ordinary man, but his mind was very revolutionary towards religious superstitions. Many talents like him always vanish from our society because geniuses are a big problem for religious bigotry. But whenever any such talent becomes famous, and when they die, Imams immediately come to perform rituals marking their Muslim connections; they don't talk about why talents like Dukhu went against them fiercely, or why they condemned him as a kafir. They know the dead can no longer rebel against them; thus, they slyly try to keep the followers of those intelligent beings on their side. Those who once denounced Dukhu Mia as an infidel now revere him as their religious guru Kazi Nazrul Islam.

Our youngsters should be vigilant against these wily religious politicians. They can change their mask at any time and will not hesitate to lick your feet if needed. They will put you in a new bottle with their old dogmas to show you have always been with them. They have great abilities and verbal techniques to destroy your natural talents.

Never will they turn towards you even if they know that you are on the right path because honesty is not a principle of fraudsters. Their sole intention is to feed themselves using religious cards.

## 3.15 Have scientists ever killed or punished someone for not believing in scientific theory? Why have religious institutions killed people for discovering the truth and not believing in a deity?

Religion is considered to be the divine truth; hence, people have blind faith in it. But when theologians punish people for revealing the truth, what divinity do they believe in?

Socrates, the teacher of many great western philosophers, could not read and write. The church sentenced him to death for his thoughts; he was accused of not believing in the gods of classical Greece. The Athenian youths were hugely fond of him, which was a real problem for the priests.

Socrates was an ancient Greek pagan — pretty much like everyone else in his society, but a fantastic individual.

He used to say that the unexamined life was not worth living. Aristotle agreed that the highest human faculty was reasoning, and its supreme activity was contemplation.

Plato gave Socrates an opportunity to escape from the prison of the Church, but Socrates' conscience refused. Rather, when he was given a deadly poison to drink, he respected the priests' orders without fear of death for his vision. This tactical cold-blooded murder in the name of divinities unquestionably exposed who acted as gods. Socrates lives no longer, but his thoughts persist in inflicting the minds of the owners of religion.

Galileo's natural studies caused him to get into serious trouble with his religious divinity because his finding was considered heretical. Consequently, his and the Church's beliefs were an example in the history of the warfare between knowledge and Christianity. At that time, he was called a natural philosopher because the term 'scientist' did not exist until the 19$^{th}$ century.

In 1616, the Catholic Church of Rome was outraged by Galileo's observations of nature. Hence, it warned him not to teach or write about his theory and banned his publications which went against the theory of God. Surprisingly, he was a devotional Christian. He respected the orders of the Fathers of the Church for fear of death. But he could no longer suffer from a delusion in exchange for a fact; thus, in 1632, he published a book of his work.

He stated that the earth revolved around the sun. But the Holy Book of God says that the earth is at the centre. The inquisition, therefore, found that Galileo was a sinner who preached that the Bible was wrong. So, he was sentenced to life imprisonment.

If Galileo's theory went against the theology of the omniscient and omnipotent deity, could he not have punished Galileo?

For discovering the truth of nature, religious scholars punish such sages! Amazingly, people still believe that these houses of God are places of holiness.

## 3.16 It is not a question of scientists against priests or vice versa, it is merely a question of truth.

If a finding is true beyond doubt, accept it and destroy the falsehood. That should be the principle of a true believer. But what is the meaning of killing the truth?

While bathing, Archimedes noticed that the water level in the tub rose as he entered; he realised its effect which led him to discover the law of nature, known as Archimedes' principle. At that time, priests would probably bathe, if not every day, once a week or month. Thus, they obviously saw the dharma (characteristic) of water every time. But they did not observe it the way he observed it. The principle that Archimedes discovered always existed in nature; but no one had read it before.

When Newton saw an apple falling from a tree, he did not run away with it. "Why does it not go up," he questions, "but come down?" This question inspired him to discover the principle of gravity.

Newton and Archimedes did not speak each other's language, but they understood the language of nature — did they not?

In ancient Egypt, people worshipped the sun god. I had been mulling this over quite a lot that those ancient people had a good sense of nature — they admired, at least with self-confidence, what was wholeheartedly admirable.

We know that the sun has no life. Suppose there is no sun anymore? The whole planet will die. Something that has no life, but it nurtures all our lives on earth!

I am sometimes so awestruck by the splendour of sunset that I cannot understand when I watch it whether I am alive or dead. Is it foolish to have the deepest admiration for the sun?

* * *

# Annex

# Annexure

## THE CONSTITUTION OF NATUROCRATIC PARTY

a party for all beings

# The Name and Principle

## 1st Article : Name

A political organisation has been created; it will be known as the Naturocratic Party. In Bengali, it will be known as প্রকৃতিতান্ত্রিক দল and in Roman letters, it may be written as Prokrititantric Daul; its members and followers may be referred to as Naturocrats or প্রকৃতিতন্ত্রবাদী. The symbol of the party will be related to its name and principles.

## 2nd Article : Principles

1. Naturocrats firmly believe and recognise that the basic foundation of any human society in the world is formed by its grassroots people; therefore, they must truly be respected, and they must have genuine political power to implement their own affairs.

2. We deeply realise that nature is the unique knowledge laboratory and provides livelihood for all beings; nature is the origin of our existence and the unique source of life; its wonderful diversity and beauty nourish our reflections, our compassion and our spiritual conviction; we are with it in life and death; we shall wholeheartedly respect nature and preserve it not only for ourselves but also for our future generations.

3. We shall establish the dispensation of justice for all living and non-living beings in harmony with nature; nature itself is a unique universal language; this is why, without distinction, literacy and illiteracy, a weaver bird and a weaver, a scientist and a poet, every being can read and understand it.

4. The natural-socio-economics shall be the core of our livelihood and happiness; to expect eternal growth in a limited space, which material-economists can

only dream of; we shall not allow a laissez-faire policy to destroy the beauty of nature and the environment in the name of development.

5. Our policies shall put individuals first and build a society of non-violence and non-interference in the affairs of others. Our main aim shall be to fulfil the aspirations of the common people: to maintain peace of mind, spiritual freedom, and universal harmony and happiness with basic needs. We shall preserve our long historical values and geo-cultural heritage, of which indigenous peoples are also an inalienable part.

6. Naturocrats profoundly value indigenous knowledge and traditions. Ecological wisdom and sustainable prosperity shall be the key areas of our political education activities. We shall no longer work against nature but together with it.

7. We believe that individual freedom is far more important than communal freedom; there is no community without the individual, but there are individuals without it; to respect the dignity of every individual is to respect the dignity of all, irrespective of the minority or the majority.

8. We shall not allow ourselves to be influenced religiously or ethnically; the colour of skin, race, tribe, creed, literacy, illiteracy, social status, minority, majority or any other prejudice shall never be the norm of our judgement.

9. We think religion is a personal matter. Each one of us always sees that everything in nature is entirely free and transparent for all beings. We shall not allow anyone, or any party to play nasty politics in the name of religion and respect all communal faiths equally like everyone's faith.

10. We believe that religious blindness and madness are the enemies of our moral goodness and happiness; any obligatory religious education shall strictly be in line with its authentic holy texts and shall not be for any financial, political or mobocratic gain.

11. We shall follow the path of good against evil with our conscience. No religious organization shall get any benefits from the state. Religion is supposed to be a divine affair, so no man can impose religious orders, punish anyone for

sins, and modify the holy book as the representative of divinity. How can those who do not understand nature tell the story of its creator?

12. We hope that no person shall be compelled to participate in any religious practice or rituals, and no one shall be barred from doing so unless it really harms or disturbs others.

13. Naturocrats value a citizen as the owner of the country. Every citizen, regardless of his or her background, community or individuality, shall enjoy all the fundamental rights and resources of the country equally. Whatever the reason, no one's citizenship can be taken away by any law.

14. We think the world is for all of us; every geographical region of this earth is unique, and so are its people, communities, cultures and nations. All human beings are alike; they are all different. We shall engage in an intercultural dialogue aimed at realising the deep sensitivity of one's beliefs and thoughts; this may help us sustain peaceful coexistence in a humane society based on wisdom and tolerance.

15. We shall sow the seeds for peaceful cooperation with all peace-loving people and nations; we recognise that all ordinary people around the globe want to live in natural peace — peace that is free from fear, threats, and conspiracies.

# Objective

### $3^{rd}$ *Article : Objectives*

The Naturocratic Party shall be a nature-inspired visionary political party — a party of dreams, ideas, and inspiration for all beings — a system of governance in harmony with nature. Naturocrats are devoted to ordinary people. We must preserve the freedom our ancestors fought for. We believe that only patriotic people can safeguard the sovereignty and integrity of their motherland.

We heartily salute and honour the memory of those who have given their lives and heart to the defence of our country, from the British colonial era to the Pakistani rule. We shall:

1. Wholeheartedly support and elect candidates of the Naturocratic Party during any parliamentary and local government elections;
2. Always serve the country and its people, whether the party is in power or not;
3. Protect and nurture our sovereignty, territorial integrity and national glory with the dignity of patriotism;
4. Always be vigilant against those who incite racism in the name of religion or otherwise; all our ethnically diverse nationalities should come together to serve the country and its environment by forming one unified happy family;
5. Always be vigilant against those who have persistently been trying to wipe out the long historical culture, language and tradition of Bengalis with ulterior motives;

6. Implement Bengali as the official language of the country and make sure that it remains so. English will only be used as an international business language. The aborigines of the country will have full right to speak their language and maintain the traditional way of life as they like;
7. Be against religious conversions through fraudulent and coercive means;
8. Encourage, educate and nurture our youngsters with wisdom, truthfulness, and honesty so that they can earn their rightful place in a decent society;
9. Initiate an effective and compulsory training programme for the youth aged 15 to 21 years so that they can spend two years in the field of natural food cultivation or patriotic volunteer organisations;
10. Re-engineer all the public services; eliminate redundant institutions or merge them with others. Honest people alone cannot do much, the system of government institutions has to be made honest;
11. Simplify the work of public administrations and ensure that accurate, complete, and clear information flows freely up to the grassroots;
12. Ensure that the bureaucrats are held individually and collectively responsible for their performance and that the bureaucracy remains transparent and fully accountable to the people;
13. Establish justice and good governance. How the country is being ruled, should get much more importance than who is ruling it;
14. Create a People's Bureau in each local administrative area, which will have the power to oversee and recommend the activities of public institutions;
15. Ensure proper utilisation and management of all resources and the treasuries of the country; strictly regulate borrowing from overseas, using public money for bureaucratic luxuries, or unproductive sectors of the economy;
16. Encourage patriotic emigrants and treat them as our own people;
17. Bring sustainable vibrancy to agro-based economies, small-scale industries, cottage enterprises, weaving, homoeopathy, and rural artisans; revitalise

traditional industries such as jute, cotton, and the informal sectors of the economy;

18. Ensure a knowledge-based economy for a self-reliant approach where environmental issues, ecological wisdom, and the fundamental needs of the ordinary people get top priority;

19. Prevent urbanisation, land acquisition, and any infrastructure works anywhere in the country without proper and long-term planning; any such feasible and optimum plans must be presented for consultations and debate before giving final authorisation;

20. Rehabilitate land reforms and distribution policies pertaining to the issues of homelessness, deforestation, and pollution; the private possession of land should be reasonably limited; illegally occupied land will be recovered; the occupants will be harshly punished;

21. Change the current educational system into a cohesive one. The academic year should be in tandem with our natural seasons. Students must think rationally and always be hungry to acquire knowledge instead of getting a degree. Educational institutions should produce a critical thinking, sensible, multilingual, and productive workforce so that students can accomplish their studies with dignity to play an active leadership role in the country or elsewhere;

22. Punish people according to their crimes, not according to their age; punishment must be very severe and must be swiftly applied in public so that no criminal and mob can get any shelter in society;

23. Respect the privacy of people and their personal lifestyle; always be aware that one's freedom does not impede the freedom of another;

24. Overseas Relations — We shall

    a. work against the destruction of the global environment in the name of modernisation and globalisation;

b. ensure that the government works in close cooperation with genuinely peace-loving and environmentally friendly countries for world peace and natural well-being;

c. cooperate fully with people across the world with the goal of completely eliminating the colonial system of imperialism;

d. propose that each continent of the world should have its own independent Peace Council. The UN should be abolished, or it can function with them as a liaison body;

e. establish close friendly relations with our neighbouring countries; forge special good relations with India and Pakistan and their people for the historical ties;

f. ensure that the government of Bangladesh sincerely cooperates with other Asian countries to safeguard Asian values and unity.

25. Abolishment of Partisan Politics

- we suggest abolishing partisan politics to create a platform for non-party system politics;

- people should develop a strong system of governance for good politics, where a person (on his or her own merits) can easily be a candidate in any electoral process of the country; the head of government may be elected for an unlimited period, having enough constitutional power to rule the country smoothly. Yet, anyone in the government or the people can challenge him or her at a reasonable time when vital issues are greatly neglected.

# Office, Collaboration and Membership

## 4th Article : Office

When the organisational activities of the party shall be launched in the future, its head or central office may be located at the residence of Shaupaun Koumar (under construction plan), 193 Ranavola Avenue, Sector-10, Uttara Model Town, Dhaka-1230, Bangladesh; until the party acquires its own office. And its overseas office may be located at his residence, 43 Harenberg, 1130 Brussels, Belgium. However, in both cases, the office can be transferred to another place at any time by the decision of the Central Council of the party.

## 5th Article : Collaboration

The Naturocratic Party shall accomplish its goals using all appropriate means of support and activity. It can also collaborate with another organisation that pursues similar goals and activities.

## 6th Article : Membership

Membership of the Naturocratic Party is open to any individual (natural person) who wholeheartedly accepts the principles or philosophy of the party, respects its aims or objectives faithfully, works willingly and strictly under its discipline, always obeys one's obligations towards the party and is not a member of any other political organization in the country.

## 7th Article : Duties of a Member:

1. Be dedicated to the party; never betray it and the country;
2. Always be truthful and faithful to yourself;

3. Live a plain life with the wisdom of nature;
4. Act in the spirit of self-sacrifice and dedication to true well-being and happiness in society;
5. Must not seek any personal gains apart from serving the party and the country, for which one will enjoy power as a respected cadre;
6. Have the mentality to work under a wise person even if the person has no formal education;
7. Be able to understand justice and apply your conscience to everyday life; remember that nepotism is the enemy of justice, avoid it when you judge something or someone;
8. Be a person of self-confidence, not a bigot. Look at an event in nature quite carefully, your lifelong learning and surprises will never end;
9. Practise constructive criticism and self-criticism; be bold in admitting one's own mistakes and shortcomings in work and in rectifying them;
10. Combat stubbornly any form of corruption in society; if religious devotees indulge in corruption, hate them the most;
11. Safeguard monolithic unity and discipline. Remain ever vigilant against the infiltration of ranks by persons not deserving of the honour of membership to the Naturocratic Party;
12. Take part in any socio-cultural and educational activities organised by the party school or any other method adopted from time to time. Train yourself in self-defence;
13. Do not make any political or policy statement on behalf of the party in public without proper consent;
14. Refrain from making false allegations or personal attacks against any fellow party officials or cadres;

15. Abide by the party's decisions, resolutions, and directives even though you might have voted against them or upheld a diverging opinion during the discussions;

16. Stand in support of the correct positions and in opposition to the incorrect ones;

17. Pay the membership dues regularly.

## 8th Article : Rights of an Effective Member:

1. To attend, discuss, and vote at relevant meetings;

2. To know about the membership records, funds, and properties of the party;

3. To put forward any request, suggestion, proposition or well-grounded criticism, and defend one's own options before reaching an agreement on the subject under discussion; in case of any disagreement with a resolution, view or policy — any such matter can be presented to a higher level, even to the Party Leader;

4. To ask for dismissal or replacement of an incompetent cadre;

5. To be elected to any relevant position in the party. The qualification of a person will be judged primarily by his or her own merits and motivation for the job. An applicant simply has to have the essential knowledge of the position; an academic degree is not necessarily required. An illiterate but correct and experienced person may be appointed for a particular position; in such a case, the person will be provided with an office assistant for his or her extra paperwork.

## 9th Article : Membership Categories and Subscriptions

There shall be the following categories of membership: Adherent Member, Effective Member, Affiliate Member, Lifelong Member, and Primary Member (only during the party's first organisational commencement period). The word 'Naturocrat' shall mean a member of any category and also a follower of the Naturocratic Party. If a person is denied membership, he or she may appeal to the appropriate organ or even to the Party Leader.

1. Adherent Member: A person who is willing to join the party shall initially apply, in a prescribed form, for an adherent membership to an appropriate local organ of the party. It shall not be obliged to give its reason for declining a membership application. An Adherent Member shall have equal rights and obligations as an Effective Member, except for voting rights. He or she may even be eligible to hold a position if approved by the concerned organ.

2. Effective Member: A good Adherent Member may normally be eligible to become an Effective Member (full member) after one year; nevertheless, the motivation and activities of the cadre during this time may be taken into account whether to review his or her case earlier or later for full membership — or whether his or her membership will be terminated. The concerned organ shall take the final decision in this regard. An Effective Member shall have voting rights.

3. Affiliate Membership: With the approval of the Leading Bureau, any professional group or other independent organization can become Affiliate Members of the Naturocratic Party without voting rights.

4. Lifelong Member: members and supporters may be conferred lifetime membership for their long, loyal or meritorious service to the party, which will be determined by the Central Council. A Lifelong Member shall automatically gain the status of an Effective Member if he or she is not already holding such status. Shaupaun Koumar, the author and architect of this constitution and founder of the Naturocratic Party, shall be deemed a lifelong member of the party as soon as its organisational activities begin.

5. Primary Member: Primary membership may be conferred to those who will make outstanding contributions by joining the party with the consent of the founder at the time of the first organisational initiation. Such members shall immediately be eligible to form the party's first Central Council and its Leading Bureau with the status of Effective Membership to their respective local organs.

6. Membership Subscription:

   a. The Leading Bureau shall from time to time determine the membership contributions as well as renewal and any other dues for all organs of the party. It may also determine subscriptions for each office bearer, committee member, and other representatives of the party.

   b. Membership needs to be renewed at the beginning of each year; if the renewal subscription is not received by the end of the first month of the year, membership is automatically cancelled.

   c. Anyone who is not capable of paying a regular contribution but is still keen to be part of the Naturocratic Party can also be or remain a member; for this purpose, a special request to the appropriate organ is needed.

   d. No person may simultaneously be a member of more than one local organ of the party.

## *10th Article : Resignation*

Each member is free to resign from the party at any time by sending his resignation letter to the competent organ.

If the member holds an office, it may be necessary to remain in office until a replacement is found.

## *11th Article : Exclusion of Membership*

The concerned organ shall have the power to expel a member whose activities are incompatible with the rules or whose behaviour causes moral or material damage to the party.

The member in question may make a motivated petition to the competent organ within 15 working days. The party shall have the right to take the final decision.

## *12th Article : Effect of cessation or exclusion*

In the event of either cessation or expulsion of a member, the person shall forfeit all rights and privileges of membership on the date of its termination, and he or she will have no further rights or claims against the party's property or funds, except for the rights or claims as a creditor.

The cessation does not exonerate the member from paying any due amount and honouring any contract with the party.

Once expelled, a member can be readmitted only after getting clearance from the party organ which approved the expulsion.

# Organisational System and Working Attitude

## 13th Article : Structure and Procedure

1. The Naturocratic Party shall have a Central Organ, which will create its Grassroots Organs in all local regions of the country.
2. The whole party must observe a unified discipline. Each organ, from grassroots upwards, shall be free to make its own internal rules and disciplines consistent with this constitution and may punish its members for disorderly conduct.
3. Foreign matters and matters that require a common policy for the entire country or a specific region shall be decided by the Central Council.
4. The lower grassroots organs are subordinated to the higher grassroots organs; all the constituent organs are subordinated and accountable to the Congress and the Central Council.
5. The Congress shall be the supreme organ and a symbol of the unity of the members of the Naturocratic Party. The Congress itself shall not act as a policy or decision-making body. It shall elect a Party Leader who will head the Central Council on which the entire power of the party will be vested.
6. At the time of the first organisational commencement, a team of a minimum of 40 persons shall be required to commence the formal functioning of the party under section 5 of Article 9.
7. The Central Council shall expand the grassroots and other local organs throughout the country and promote the principles, objectives, and platform

of the organisation; a grassroots organ, together with other units, shall encourage, coordinate, and support this.

8. The formation and dissolution of a grassroots organ shall be decided by its corresponding higher grassroots organ. The basic organs shall consist of different categories of people in rural and urban areas.

9. All decisions shall be made by a majority vote of those who are present and voting, except as specifically stated elsewhere in this constitution.

10. A natural or an open voting system, with no hidden ballot, shall usually apply in most cases.

## *14th Article : Central and Grassroots Organs*

The Naturocratic Party shall have a Congress and a Central Council that will have a Leading Bureau and a CoreBody. The party shall also have grassroots organs.

## *15th Article : Congress*

1. The Congress shall be the supreme authority with the power to review, ratify, amend or revoke any decisions made by the Central Council (CC) or any other organs of the party.

2. The number of delegates to Congress and the procedure for governing their election shall be determined by the Central Council.

3. An ordinary session of Congress shall be held once in every five years. In unforeseeable circumstances, it may be held earlier or postponed later. It shall be convened by the CC about two months prior to the session of Congress indicating the time, day, date, and venue with its proposed agenda.

4. An extraordinary Congress may be convened at the request of the Central Council, the Party Leader or at least one-third grassroots members of the whole party; a month's notice shall normally be required for such a meeting.

5. The Congress shall elect a leader of the party for an unlimited period from its voting delegates. The Party Leader (section 5 of Article 13) shall choose the members of the CoreBody and Leading Bureau of the Central Council. He or

she shall also head the Central Security and Disciplinary Guard, which shall be elected by the CC. The Leading Bureau shall have a Secretariat which will be responsible for the day-to-day administrative affairs. There shall be a Central Wisdom and Justice Commission that will act as an independent advisory body to the whole party.

6. Congress shall have the power to adopt and amend the constitution, which will require a majority of two-thirds of the vote; its principle, i.e., to amend Article 2 of this constitution and remove the Party Leader from power would require three-fourths of the vote, two-thirds of the representatives present. He or she shall be eligible for re-election.

7. The quorum of the Congress shall be a simple majority of its voting delegates.

## 16th Article : Central Council (CC)

1. The Central Council shall be the party's sole policy-making body. It shall be responsible for directing the entire work in accordance with the principles and objectives of the Party Constitution. It shall have ultimate authority in all matters.

2. A minimum of five years of good party membership and at least 40 years of age shall be eligible for membership in the CC. This stipulation may only be relaxed in very exceptional cases.

3. The Central Council shall have a Leading Bureau of about 21 to 25 full members, with a CoreBody of about five to seven full members; the CoreBody shall be the highest authority of the leadership of the Naturocratic Party.

4. The CC shall meet in a plenary session at least once a year; in the session, the Leading Bureau shall present its annual report. Extraordinary sessions may be held as often as required and requested by the Party Leader, or at the requisition of two-thirds of its members. General meetings usually require a thirty-day notice period, and emergency meetings may take place at short notice without formal communication.

5. The Leading Bureau and its CoreBody shall exercise the functions and powers of the CC when the CC will not be in the plenary session.

6. The CC shall determine the most suitable way for party cadres to promote political education and progress.

7. At the time of a congressional session, the constituent central organs and leaders shall continue their regular day-to-day work until a new Central Council is formed.

8. The CC and the Party Leader shall have the power to expel or take any punitive action against a member for gross misconduct or violation of the constitution or breach of discipline.

9. It shall lay down rules and conditions for a parliamentary or election committee so that they can nominate candidates for the party during any parliamentary and local government elections in the country. In such cases, Naturocrat candidates for any legislative body shall be chosen by the appropriate grassroots organ subject to approval by the CC. Naturocrats who may be elected as members of the country's national or local legislature must comply with the conditions and decisions of the Naturocratic Party.

10. The Leading Bureau shall be responsible for the immediate and at the same time transmitting the party's decisions, programmes, and vital information to all grassroots organs. It shall solve their problems in time.

11. It may appoint party officials and cadres for conducting missions abroad on the recommendation of the department concerned.

12. It shall regulate and supervise the use and maintenance of party funds of the central and local organs.

13. It shall periodically render accounts of its own work and the secretariat to the CC.

14. The quorum of the Central Council shall be a simple majority of its members. No quorum shall be necessary for adjourned meetings.

## 17th Article : Grassroots Organs

A grassroots organ, during its formation, shall follow a similar procedure and pattern of the central organ but within its jurisdiction.

## 18th Article : Working Attitude of Officials

1. Committees at all levels of the party shall function under a team leadership based on the wisdom of labour, including individual responsibilities.

2. The party's policy shall not be for rotational use of power. Officers shall have sufficient power to do their job diligently without unnecessary bureaucratic hurdles, but not to misuse power. They shall be personally and collectively accountable for their work only during the period of their tenure.

3. Each organ and department shall periodically prepare an effective report and continuously try to improve work efficiency, both technically and manually.

4. All resolutions and orders of the central organs shall be signed by the competent officer and countersigned by the Party Leader or otherwise if approved.

5. Preferably twice a year, all local organs shall forward their up-to-date membership lists and periodic reports to the Leading Bureau of the Central Council.

# Finance and the Rest

## *19th Article : Finance*

1. The party shall be financed largely by regular contributions from its members and well-wishers as well as from various activities.
2. The Central Council (CC) shall be responsible for party funding and management. The CC will establish rules and regulations to ensure periodic scrutiny of revenues and funds and other assets of the entire party. It will generate an annual budget and allocate funds accordingly.
3. The property and revenue of the Naturocratic Party shall be applied solely to the promotion of its objectives, and no portion thereof shall be distributed among its members as dividends, except for a bona fide compensation for the services rendered or expenses incurred on behalf of the party.
4. At least two officials from among the Central Treasurer, Deputy Leaders, Leader, or other authorised persons shall sign all legal documents on behalf of the party.
5. The financial accounts of the party's expenditure and revenue shall be audited by a board of audit.
6. The party's financial year shall begin on July 1 and end on June 30 each year.

## 20th Article : Duration

The party has been created for an indefinite duration.

## 21st Article : Winding up

In the event of the party winding up, the assets available after the settlement of its debts and liabilities shall not be distributed among its members, rather, they shall be donated to any other organisation which has similar objectives.

## 22nd Article : No right to use the name 'Naturocratic'

No person or faction of the party shall have the right to use the name 'Naturocratic' or 'Naturocrat' in order to create a separate or different political entity than this Naturocratic Party.

## 23rd Article : Null and Void

If any article or section of this statute shall become contrary to the laws of the country, its article or section shall be considered null and void.

# Provisions

### *24th Article : Enforcement*

This constitution may be enforced from the day the party's organisational activities begin.

Brussels, January 20, 2009

Shaupaun Koumar

Printed by Libri Plureos GmbH in Hamburg,
Germany